Please check all items for damages
before leaving the Library.
Thereafter you will be held
responsible for all injuries
to items beyond reasonable wear.

BUILDING
EMOTIONAL
INTELLIGENCE

Also by Linda Lantieri

Schools with Spirit:
Nurturing the Inner Lives of Children and Teachers

Waging Peace in Our Schools

BUILDING EMOTIONAL INTELLIGENCE

Techniques to Cultivate Inner Strength in Children

LINDA LANTIERI

Introduction and Guided Practices by
DANIEL GOLEMAN

SOUNDS TRUE
Boulder, Colorado

PARENT
TEACHER
155.4124
LAN

Sounds True, Inc., Boulder CO 80306

© 2008 Linda Lantieri
© 2008 Introduction by Daniel Goleman

Published 2008

Printed in Canada

⊕ This book is printed on recycled paper containing 100% post-consumer waste and processed without chlorine.

10 9 8 7 6 5 4 3 2

Library of Congress Cataloging-in-Publication Data

Lantieri, Linda.
  Building emotional intelligence : techniques to cultivate inner strength in children / Linda Lantieri ; introduction and practices guided by Daniel Goleman.
      p. cm.
Includes bibliographical references.
ISBN 978-1-59179-789-0 (hardcover)
1. Emotional intelligence--Study and teaching. 2. Emotions in children--Study and teaching. I. Title.

BF576.L37 2008
155.4'124--dc22
                            2008000576

Book design by Karen Polaski

This book is dedicated to my mother, whose life rich in purpose and meaning introduced me to the importance of having a regular contemplative practice. Mom — you were so ahead of your time, and you would be thrilled to see this book published, as it will help many more children, parents, and teachers to carry out what you taught me.

CONTENTS

Acknowledgments

The idea for this book and CD started to take form in March 2007 at one of the many lively and inspiring lunches Daniel Goleman and I have had over the years. Dan's wisdom, generosity of spirit, and willingness to be an integral part of this project were what made this book possible. One of the things I appreciate most about my friendship with Dan is his uncanny ability to discern just when he needs to generously offer his support and know-how to a project. His spontaneous acts of kindness usually have the ripple effect of benefiting the lives of countless adults and children. I extend my deepest admiration and gratitude to you, Dan. I am sure this book would not have reached fruition if you had not answered your inner call to be involved with it.

When Sounds True graciously offered to publish *Building Emotional Intelligence* and Hanuman Goleman willingly agreed to produce the CD, I knew only that I was to be an instrument to help this project happen. It took a leap of faith into the unknown because I couldn't quite envision yet where I would find the time or the wisdom necessary to do justice to the task at hand. Luckily, when I said yes to this offer, I was met with abundance in terms of the people and resources needed to make this project possible. I would like to thank the following individuals in my life and work.

I am most grateful to the hundreds of administrators, teachers, parents, and children in the twelve schools in and around the area in lower Manhattan that is now referred to as Ground Zero. You trusted me enough to be willing to try out the strategies presented in this book at a time when you were most vulnerable. I feel privileged that you gave me the gift of being a part of your healing and recovery process.

I feel particularly indebted also to my staff at the Inner Resilience Program: Charlotte de Lucia, Dragica Mikavica, Dana McCloskey, and Veronica Vieira. As I took time away from the daily responsibilities at hand, you maintained the quality of the work we needed to bring to hundreds of children, parents, and teachers. Thank you all for your loving support and encouragement throughout.

I want to express my gratitude to those adults and children who piloted this particular version of the materials presented here—and you did it on such short notice. First to the parents: Martha Eddy, Susanne Harnett, Lynne Hurdle-Price, Laura Parker Roerden, Elsa Punset Bannel, and Marilyn Zlotnik; and to the children they piloted these strategies with: Arielle Diker, Ian and Katherine Harnett, Gabriel and Samantha Hultberg, Eli Parker Roerden, Nai'im and Jabari Hurdle-Price, Sekai Hurdle, and Alexia Jimenez de Punset. Thank you for making the final product so much more relevant because of your useful feedback.

I also want to express my deep appreciation to three colleagues and friends who helped in different ways to transform my earlier drafts into a polished manuscript worthy of the topic it addresses. I could not have successfully completed this project without the steady support and skill of Neeta Jain, Laura Parker Roerden, and Tom Roepke. Thank you for being so deeply involved throughout this process.

My gratitude also is extended to my newfound family at Sounds True, especially editorial director Kelly Notaras and editor Stephen Topping, whose helpful assistance was there throughout. Thank you for honoring my process even when it meant slowing down the timeline.

I am also grateful to those colleagues and mentors who share this journey with me of making social and emotional learning and nurturing the inner life an integral part of children's experience at home and in school. Thank you especially to Roger Weissberg, Mary Utne O'Brien, Mark Greenberg, Timothy Shriver, Tom Roderick, Maurice Elias, Parker Palmer, Angeles Arrien, Sue Keister, Richard Davidson, Jon Kabat-Zinn, Tobin Hart, Peter Yarrow, and Marian Wright Edelman. Your example is a constant inspiration for me to live my life and work to the fullest.

I have a powerful team of family and close friends in my life that I have a deep spiritual kinship with and who are part of my soul family. My deepest thanks to Carmella B'Hahn, Elaine Seiler, Robin Stern, Janet Patti, Madhavi Nambiar, Jezabella Kipp, Linda Loffredo, Mariano Guzmán, Eileen Rockefeller Growald, Nancy Carlsson-Paige, Martha Eddy, Lynne Hurdle-Price, Amshatar Monroe, Rosalind Winter, and my sister Lois Corbett. You, my dear "soul friends," are my compassionate witness to my inner life of mind and spirit and my outer life of action and service. I am grateful for your unconditional love, wisdom, and inner strength.

Finally my deepest gratitude for the love and support of the NoVo Foundation for recognizing how important it was that this work continue. I will always be grateful that you answered the call.

— *Linda Lantieri*
2008

Introduction

BY DANIEL GOLEMAN

Recently I spoke with a mother about how her daughter was doing in school. "Well," she said, "she's good at math, better at English—but even better at emotional intelligence."

That was a conversation that could not have occurred just a while ago. It was 1993 when Linda Lantieri and I, along with a small group of like-minded colleagues, got together to establish the Collaborative for Academic, Social, and Emotional Learning (CASEL). Back then there were but a handful of programs that exemplified the best promise of "social emotional learning" (SEL), the systematic classroom teaching of emotional intelligence. These programs add to the regular school day a curriculum for handling life: improving self-awareness and confidence, managing disturbing emotions and impulses, increasing empathy and cooperation.

Linda was at the helm of one of those programs, Resolving Conflict Creatively, which had already found its way into hundreds of schools as a way to fight rising rates of violence. Many of the early social and emotional learning efforts in schools were developed to combat just such a challenge: teens' use of drugs and alcohol, dropouts, unwanted teen pregnancies, and other pitfalls of adolescence. When the W. T. Grant Foundation commissioned a study of all such programs to see what actually made some of them work (while others did not), the teaching of social and emotional skills emerged among the crucial active ingredients.

Over the years since Linda and I first worked together, social and emotional learning has spread to tens of thousands of schools worldwide, and it continues to grow. Some of that growth was helped along by my 1995 book *Emotional Intelligence,* which argued that schools would better equip children for life if the curriculum included not just the academic basics, but also coaching in the basics of social and emotional competence. A heightened self-awareness, better ability to manage distressing emotions, increased sensitivity to how others feel, and managing relationships well are vital throughout life. But the foundation for these life competencies is laid in childhood.

Brain science tells us that a child's brain goes through major growth that does not end until the mid-twenties. Neuroplasticity, as scientists call it, means that the sculpting of the brain's circuitry during this period of brain growth depends to a great degree on what a child experiences day-to-day. During this window these environmental influences on brain growth are particularly powerful in shaping a child's social and emotional neural circuits. Children who are well nurtured and whose parents help them learn how to calm down when they are upset, for instance, seem to develop greater strength in the brain's circuits for managing distress; those whose parents neglect them will be more likely to act on aggressive impulses or have trouble calming down when they are upset.

Good parents are like good teachers. By offering a secure base, the caring adults in children's lives can create an environment that lets children's brains function at their best. That base becomes a safe haven, a zone of strength from which they can venture forth to explore, to master something new, to achieve. That secure base can become internalized when children are taught to better manage their anxiety and so more keenly focus their attention. This enhances their ability to reach an optimal zone for learning as well.

One way to ensure every child gets the best lessons of the heart is to make them part of the school day as well part of a child's home life. As I noted earlier, Linda and I are founding members of the

Collaborative for Academic, Social, and Emotional Learning, an organization based at the University of Illinois at Chicago that has set standards for SEL and helped school systems around the world bring these programs into their curriculum. The best social and emotional learning programs in schools are designed to fit seamlessly into the standard school curriculum for children at every age.

The question is, does social and emotional learning make a difference in children's lives? Now we have the answer: a definitive meta-analysis of more than one hundred studies compared students who had SEL with those who did not. The data shows impressive improvements among the SEL students in their behavior in and out of the classroom. Students not only mastered abilities like calming down and getting along better, but they also learned more effectively; their grades improved, and their scores on academic achievement tests were a hefty fourteen percentile points higher than similar students who were not given such social and emotional learning programs.[1] Helping children master their emotions and relationships makes them better learners.

Why helping children handle their inner world and relationships better boosts learning can be understood, too, in terms of the impact of SEL on children's developing neural circuitry. One area of the brain most shaped by experience during childhood is the prefrontal cortex, the brain's executive center. This area holds the circuits both for inhibiting disruptive emotional impulses and for paying attention — for calming and focusing. When children do not have strategies for decreasing their anxiety, less attention is available to them to learn, solve problems, and grasp new ideas. A child, for example, who gets panicked by a pop quiz, will actually imprint that response rather than the details of any material in the quiz. Distress kills learning. Scientists now believe that improving attention and memory, along with freeing the mind from impulsivity and distress, puts a child's mind in the best zone for learning. And social and emotional learning does just that.

Linda Lantieri has continued to be a pioneer in the movement to integrate social and emotional learning into schools throughout the world. Currently she has been facing one of education's greatest challenges: how to help children who have suffered a shock like the events of 9/11 become more resilient, so they can bounce back from trauma and get on with their lives and education. Working with children in the schools closest to the former World Trade Center, Linda has developed a curriculum that can help any child calm the body, quiet the mind, and pay better attention.

These are skills that all children need, not just in school, but throughout life. Parents and teachers tell children countless times to "calm down," or "pay attention." But the natural course of a child's development means that the brain's circuitry for calming and focusing is a work in progress: those neural systems are still growing. Yet we can help them along by giving children systematic lessons that will strengthen these budding capacities. That's what Linda has done in her state-of-the-art curriculum in the New York City Schools, and what she offers any family or classroom here in this book and CD set.

When Linda asked if I would narrate the instructional exercises that teach these skills, I jumped at the chance. I'm honored to once again be involved with Linda Lantieri's groundbreaking work, this time as the voice that narrates the instructional CDs. And I'm delighted by the thought of the many children whose lives will benefit from this practical wisdom.

CHAPTER 1

※☼※

Building Inner Preparedness

In downtown Manhattan on the morning of September 11, 2001, nobody could have predicted that within hours more than five thousand schoolchildren and two hundred teachers would be running for their lives. It was only the sixth day of school, and most classrooms were already well into their morning routines: unpacking book bags, saying hello to friends. In fact, when the first loud crash occurred, the sound didn't even seem that unfamiliar for New York City on a busy fall morning. Most teachers went on with their morning routines. Then there was the second sound that shook most of the buildings nearby and reverberated for blocks. And some saw what was happening right outside their classroom window. Principals and teachers started to get fragmented information as to what was happening. They soon realized that they were caught in the middle of an unimaginable event as thousands of children were anxiously looking to them to make sense out of what was happening.

Somehow the adults in charge knew that the only way they were going to be able to make the right decisions was to stay calm and help their children do the same. Most schools gathered their children in the gyms or cafeterias. They passed out crayons and paper to students who began to draw pictures of what they had already seen before the shades were drawn. They were drawing pictures of the

twin towers with what they thought were birds and butterflies falling from the windows.

The adults had so little to go on in terms of what to do. Their
supervisors were advising them to do various things before all communication was cut off. But those supervisors were more than a mile
away and really couldn't imagine what these teachers and principals were seeing firsthand. In the midst of profound uncertainty and
danger, these adults had to make the ultimate decision of their careers
as educators: saving the children would have to mean evacuating the
school and running to safety.

Once they got outside, many were engulfed in a black cloud of dust
as children walked and ran hand-in-hand, with some teachers leading them in familiar chants and rhymes to take the children's minds
off what they were seeing and hearing. Many of the women teachers took off their high heels in order to run faster. As one third-grade
teacher said: "The two eight-year-olds who were holding my hands
ran as fast as I could. I'm not sure what kept me going as I hurtled
forward in that river of running. . . . I would remember a day or two
later that a child said to me, 'Look! Even the dogs are scared.'"

Miraculously, though debris fell around them and confusion
reigned, not a single student or teacher's life was lost. In that moment,
the adults in children's lives accessed the inner wisdom, courage, and
calm it took to successfully evacuate whole schools of young children
safely. Children who saw unspeakable sights somehow managed to
persevere on their long march to safety that day and, grappling to
make meaning out of disaster, imagined that bodies falling from the
twin towers were birds in flight.[1]

What got these remarkable adults and children through that day
was not how well those children had performed on the last stan-
dardized test they took. That day, facing the deepest tests of life, the
question of academic preparedness took a backseat to the question of
inner preparedness. Somehow enough principals, teachers, and students had the inner resources to connect to their deeper wisdom. In

the midst of the devastation around them, they were able to remain calm and balanced. It was from such an internal state of relaxed alertness that they were able to make the right decisions that would lead them all to safety.

Having been in Manhattan on that day and being among those who came to support the teachers and students of Ground Zero, I had some profound realizations. I became more deeply aware that the real tests of life can come a child's way at any moment, and that we as adults cannot protect our children from circumstances beyond our control. The question instead has become how to equip children with the inner strength they need to meet both the intense challenges and the great opportunities that come their way. Can we, in fact, cultivate the "ways of being" that helped both students and teachers at Ground Zero maintain calm and balance in the midst of such profound uncertainty and unknowing?

While certainly it could be argued that the teachers and children that day exhibited the inner resources they needed, what would it take to refill the well from which they had drawn so deeply? As the modern stresses of today's childhood accumulate in children, how can we cultivate the habits of mind, body, and heart it will take to continually relieve the pressure?

As children in the schools at Ground Zero reflected on their year in late June 2002, one young boy in an elementary school a block from the former World Trade Center looked at his teacher straight in the eye and said, "I'll never forget that on that day you held my hand, and you didn't let go." Those of us who are raising our children have to remember how important it is to nurture our own inner lives so that we can offer our children the kinds of support they need to develop their inner strength. We must not let go until we have helped our children feel that inner security.

WHAT THIS GUIDE IS ABOUT

Since September 11, 2001, I have been involved in equipping thousands of children and adults with the skills and strategies that help them quiet their minds, calm their bodies, and identify and manage their emotions more effectively. As founder and director of the Inner Resilience Program (formerly Project Renewal), I have seen that the capacity to be more in control of one's thoughts, emotions, and physiology can form a sort of internal armor that gives children the inner preparedness they need to face the challenges and opportunities of life.

This book offers some practical ideas and strategies for both you and the children in your care to develop the ability to appreciate silence and stillness by taking regular moments of quiet time together, and to become more skillful in managing stress. It presents an opportunity for you to give your family a scheduled time to bring balance, replenishment, and calmness into your lives. Patrice Thomas, in her book *The Power of Relaxation,* writes about a designated quiet time with children as "heart and soul time."[2] You can decide what you want to call it and even involve children in choosing a name.

The important point is that you are deciding to have this regular "heart and soul time" as a part of your family's routine. Secondly, in using the CD and accompanying material, you are providing the opportunity to develop some concrete skills in cultivating both your and your child's inner strength and emotional intelligence.

Depending on the age of your child (or children), this journey will be different. Young children, for example, still have a great capacity to access the inner dimensions you will explore here. They still have the ability to see beneath the surface of things. They are full of wonder and awe and can play creatively. Sometimes they can sense things that adults often take time to perceive or know. For example, young children are able to make quick intuitive decisions about whom they will be friendly with. However, when this aspect of a child is not affirmed and noticed, it becomes hidden and repressed. As a result, young children can lose touch with a part of themselves that is already quite well developed.

Sadly, as children move through their childhood, they often receive messages—spoken and unspoken—that the extraordinary experiences of their inner lives are not honored as part of their reality. They begin to think that they can't possibly know something intuitively or have deep compassion for someone, because they just aren't old enough. As children grow up, the more repressed, forgotten, and locked within themselves the awareness of their inner life becomes. Adolescence offers an opportunity to reopen this line of inquiry, yet young people at this stage are usually met by the adult tendency to ignore or trivialize transcendental experiences. What complicates matters is that few of us have experienced being nurtured in these ways ourselves. If we hope to be a part of cultivating this approach with our children, we will each need to find positive models and experiences that can show us how to live in a more integrated way.

We suggest that you start doing this kind of work with children as young as five years old. Children this age are looking for cues from parents about what is safe to explore and what is not. Doing these exercises with children of any age gives them a clear message that we value and recognize their inner capacities. And it is important to do them regularly to get the benefits that they can provide. The goal is to bring stillness and balance, through the use of these techniques, to every aspect of your life and your child's life. Although this book talks about parents taking the lead in teaching these skills to children at home, teachers also can offer these strategies in the classroom setting. All of the suggestions and approaches in this book are equally applicable and adaptable to both the home and school environment.

I have chosen to focus on two techniques in this book and CD for building inner resilience and enhancing emotional intelligence in children:

1. Relaxing the body (through progressive muscle relaxation and a body scan exercise)

2. Focusing the mind (through a mindfulness exercise)

This chapter describes some of the benefits of teaching children to have a regular practice of stillness, and it includes a review of some of the research that informs the work.

Chapter 2 provides some guiding principles, and it focuses on the role of the adult in creating the welcoming learning environment necessary for this work to flourish.

Chapters 3, 4, and 5 are separate chapters for each of the following age groups: ages five to seven, eight to eleven, and twelve years and up. Each chapter includes exercises, tailored to the proper age group, to do both before and after listening to the CD. The CD itself offers a guided contemplative practice, led by Daniel Goleman, appropriate for the age of your child.

Finally, Chapter 6 summarizes some of the steps that can be taken to ensure the long-term sustainability of these efforts on behalf of children.

The ideas and strategies presented here are not meant to be the solution to the various educational, behavioral, and health concerns children face. However, it is helpful for children and adults to have inner mechanisms available that reduce the body's stress reaction itself. Some of these benefits for both you and the children in your care include:

- Increased self-awareness and self-understanding
- Greater ability to relax the body and release physical tension
- Improved concentration and ability to pay attention, which is critical to learning
- The ability to deal with stressful situations more effectively by creating a more relaxed way of responding to stressors
- Greater control over your thoughts, with less domination by unwelcome thoughts
- Greater opportunity for deeper communication and understanding between parent and child, because you are sharing your thoughts and feelings on a regular basis

As you begin this journey of taking a regular quiet time with each of your children, we hope there will be benefits to you as well. You are likely to develop a heightened level of self-awareness and have a deeper understanding of who your child is. As you take these set times to be fully present with your child in a very different way than you have before, you may find that you are able to bring a new level of present-moment awareness to other parts of your day. I hope it will help you become more available to yourself and your children in general so that you, too, can cope more successfully with life's stressors and enjoy the heart and soul of parenting.

WHAT THE RESEARCH HAS TO SAY ABOUT TEACHING CALMING EXERCISES TO REDUCE STRESS AND ENHANCE WELL-BEING

The severity of unmanaged stress in our society is evident. It is estimated that 70 to 90 percent of all doctor visits in the United States today are for stress-related disorders.[3] In a ten-year study, people who were unable to manage stress effectively were shown to have a death rate 40 percent higher than that of nonstressed individuals.[4] Our society is bent on quick fixes when life challenges come our way. We medicate ourselves and our children. Americans consume five billion tranquilizers every year in an effort to control their stress.[5]

Children's lives are much more stressful today as well. When adults live at a hurried, frenetic pace, their children are at the receiving end. Our society itself, in the United States, has changed in many ways that increase pressure on children and compromise their childhood. Many parents are working longer hours and are allowing work to intrude on their lives anywhere and everywhere. As a result, more children are spending substantial amounts of time with multiple caregivers. There is a constant push for children to achieve at academic skills earlier, and so school becomes a big source of stress in their lives.

Too many young people today are experiencing mental health and adjustment difficulties, and our society doesn't spend the resources to provide appropriate help and attention. It is estimated that one out of five nine- to seventeen-year-olds has a diagnosable mental disorder.[6] The fact is that an increasing number of children are entering schools in crisis, unprepared cognitively and emotionally to learn. At the same time, educators confront the challenge of higher public expectations while dealing with diminishing internal resources to do their jobs well.

We often mistake the symptoms of unmanaged stress in our children as inappropriate behavior that needs to be stopped. Children are reprimanded by teachers and parents for actions that are really stress reactions, rather than intentional misbehavior. The situation becomes a downward spiral of one stress reaction after another, and both adult and child are caught in it.

A poll conducted by the national Kids Poll surveyed 875 children, ages nine through thirteen, about what caused them stress and what coping strategies they used the most to deal with the stress in their lives. The top three sources of stress that they reported were grades, school, and homework (36 percent); family (32 percent); and friends, peers, gossip, and teasing (21 percent). The top three coping strategies were to play or do something active (52 percent); to listen to music (44 percent); and to watch TV or play a video game (42 percent). Of the ten coping strategies that were chosen the most, not one involved going within or being contemplative, such as the strategies we will explore in this book. The good news, however, is that 75 percent of those surveyed reported the need for their parents to spend time with them when they are going through a difficult time.[7] This may help as you approach your child in trying out some of these techniques. These strategies will not only help manage their stress better, but also provide them with some quality time with you.

Our experience as children was vastly different from the world our children face. Today's world includes all kinds of stressors that didn't even exist when we were growing up. As an elementary teacher during the 1970s and later as an administrator in New York City Schools, I started to notice that young people's social and emotional development seemed to be on a serious decline. I was seeing children coming to school more aggressive, more disobedient, more impulsive, more sad, more lonely. In fact, psychologist Thomas Achenbach, from the University of Vermont, confirmed my observations. His groundbreaking study of thousands of American children, first in the mid-1970s and then again in the late 1980s, proved this to be true. America's children—from the poorest to the most affluent—displayed a decline across the board in their scores on over forty measures designed to reflect a variety of emotional and social capacities.[8]

The dominant paradigm in response to this decline in children's social and emotional capacities focused on trying to identify the risk factors that caused this antisocial behavior. There were almost two decades of school-based "prevention wars," like the "war on drugs," to help reduce the negative behavior. In the last two decades we have witnessed a healthy paradigm shift. Researchers and practitioners are studying the concept of resilience—the innate ability we all have to self-correct and thrive in the face of life's challenges. Bonnie Bernard, a pioneer in the field of strength-based approaches, has helped us take a look at how young people's strengths and capabilities can be developed in order to protect them from the potential harm that these circumstances represent.[9] This body of research has direct relevance as we think about cultivating inner strength in children through giving them a regular practice of quieting their minds and calming their bodies.

The resilience-building research also points to one of the most important protective factors a child can have: the presence of at least one caring and supportive adult (ideally several) who believes in the worth of the child. Children need the adults in their lives to be steady anchors who never give up on them. They also need to learn concrete social and emotional skills, taught both in the home and at school, and they need lots of opportunities to practice those skills so that they become available whenever the child needs to use them. The materials in this book strengthen all three of the above conditions.

What do we know specifically about the benefits of systematically teaching adults and children to relax their bodies and focus their minds as a way of building resilience? Hundreds of studies have been published, some in peer-reviewed journals, of the benefits (in particular) of the calming technique called Mindfulness-Based Stress Reduction (MBSR) through the work of Jon Kabat-Zinn, who founded the Stress Reduction Program at the University of Massachusetts Medical School. Kabat-Zinn first studied the use of mindfulness technique with adult patients suffering from chronic pain. He found that patients not only reported a decrease of pain, but also that their blood pressure decreased, and they reported an increased sense of well-being. Today, forms of MBSR are being used in more than two hundred medical centers around the country, for treating not only chronic pain but also cardiovascular disease and the effects of cancer therapy.[10]

Kabat-Zinn also conducted a study with psoriasis patients and found that those who were taught a mindfulness meditation practice healed four times faster than the control group. In 2001, Kabat-Zinn studied people who did not have a major medical problem but certainly had their share of the everyday stresses of life. In this study, the volunteers were randomly assigned to either the control or treatment group. The treatment group was taught and asked to practice exercises that included the two calming strategies presented in this book and CD: mindfulness meditation and body scans. The intervention also included yoga. After three months, the group who practiced these calming strategies regularly showed a 46 percent decrease in medical symptoms such as colds, headaches, etc.; a 44 percent decrease in psychological distress; and a 24 percent reduction in the stress response to everyday hassles. The control group showed no significant change in their levels of stress.[11]

Dr. Richard Davidson, professor of psychology and psychiatry at the University of Wisconsin in Madison, has also been adding to the research about the benefits of teaching these calming strategies to adults. Through various studies he has conducted over the years on the effects of meditation, we now know that these strategies increase the gray matter in the brain, improve the immune system, reduce stress, and promote a sense of well-being. A more recent study conducted by Dr. Davidson attempted to examine how meditation affects attention. Since meditation can be thought of as a kind of mental training of attention, he decided to examine whether meditation could have a significant impact on performance requiring attentional abilities. He found out that attention seems to be a flexible, trainable skill. Those participants who had three months of intensive meditation experience were able to do better on a test of attention called the attentional blink. He decided to use the attentional blink to explore the connection of meditation to attention because it was considered to be a fixed property of the nervous system. However, Dr. Davidson's beginning research points to the idea that attention can improve with practice. This new discovery may have some profound implications for children and learning.[12]

Until a short time ago, most of the research into the effects of these kinds of practices has been conducted on adults. More rigorous scientific research began in approximately 2006 — using measurable data that could produce reproducible results — on the effects of these calming techniques on children. Today several studies are under way throughout the United States and Canada. The Inner Resilience Program, which I founded and direct, is one such research effort. Through the services of Metis Associates, Inc., we are conducting original empirical research using an experimental design that will examine the impact our services have on a select group of New York City teachers, students, and classrooms. Sixty participants are in the study — half in the treatment group and half in the control group. As part of our intervention, teachers are exposed to the calming techniques included in this book, and then they are taught how to teach these skills to their students using our curriculum, "Building Resilience from the Inside Out — Grades K–12."

Several of us who are embarking on this more rigorous scientific research are encouraged by preliminary anecdotal findings. Many of us who have been teaching these skills to children have been heartened by some of the changes we've noticed. For example, Kimberly Schonert-Reichl, from the University of Columbia in Canada, observed that children who were taught a mindfulness technique similar to the one in this book were "less aggressive; less oppositional toward teachers; more attentive in class; and reported more positive emotions including more optimism." Susan Smalley, director of the

Mindfulness Awareness Research Center at UCLA, also found positive results from teaching these techniques to teenagers with attention deficit hyperactivity disorder (ADHD). She found that learning mindfulness techniques reduced their anxiety and increased their ability to focus. Several other, more rigorous, scientific studies are under way. In the meantime, many of us are continuing to experience firsthand the benefits this kind of approach can have for children.[13]

THE DEVELOPMENT OF SOCIAL AND EMOTIONAL COMPETENCIES[14]

A growing body of research suggests that helping children develop good social and emotional skills early in life makes a big difference in their long-term health and well-being. Studies have shown that children's social and emotional functioning and behavior begin to stabilize around the age of eight, and can predict the state of their behavior and mental health later in life.[15] In other words, if children learn to express emotions constructively and engage in caring and respectful relationships before and while they are in the lower elementary grades, they are more likely to avoid depression, violence, and other serious mental health problems as they grow older.

Daniel Goleman, who guides us in the calming practices on the CD that accompanies this book, has contributed much to our thinking about the need to nurture the social and emotional lives of children. Today there are hundreds of efforts all over the world to teach children social and emotional skills as part of their school curriculum.

In his groundbreaking book *Emotional Intelligence* (published in 1995), Goleman summarized the research from the fields of neuroscience and cognitive psychology that identified EQ—emotional intelligence—as being as important as IQ in terms of children's healthy development and future life success. He wrote:

> One of psychology's open secrets is the relative inability of grades, IQ, or SAT scores, despite their popular mystiques, to predict unerringly who will succeed in life. . . . There are widespread exceptions to the rule that IQ predicts success—many (or

more) exceptions than cases that fit the rule. At best, IQ contrib-
utes about 20 percent to the factors that determine life success,
which leaves 80 percent to other forces.[16]

Goleman's work helped educators, including myself, understand
the importance of emotional intelligence as a basic requirement for
the effective use of one's IQ—that is, one's cognitive skills and knowledge. He made the connection between our feelings and our thinking
more explicit by pointing out how the brain's emotional and executive areas are interconnected physiologically, especially as these areas
relate to teaching and learning. The prefrontal lobes of the brain,
which control emotional impulses, are also where working memory
resides and where all learning takes place.

Educators and parents alike are now much more aware that
when chronic anxiety, anger, or upset feelings intrude on children's
thoughts, less capacity is available in working memory to process
what they are trying to learn. This implies that, at least in part, academic success depends on a student's ability to maintain positive
social interactions. Schools across the country today are systematically helping children strengthen their EQs by equipping them with
concrete skills for identifying and managing their emotions, commu-
nicating effectively, and resolving conflicts nonviolently. These skills
help children to make good decisions, to be more empathetic, and to
be optimistic in the face of setbacks.

The hopeful news is that schools and parents, working together,
can play pivotal roles in supporting children's healthy development
in dealing with their emotions and in their relationships with others.
This is referred to as *social and emotional learning* (SEL) because these
are indeed skills that can be learned and mastered, every bit as much
as language or mathematics or reading can be. Furthermore, teaching
academic skills and social and emotional skills is not an either/or prop-
osition. In fact, there is a great deal of research evidence to indicate that
students perform better when academics are combined with SEL.[17]

What are these crucial skills? In 1995, Daniel Goleman, Eileen Rockefeller Growald, Timothy Shriver, myself, and others founded the Collaborative for Academic, Social, and Emotional Learning, an organization that focuses on the use of SEL as an essential part of education. CASEL lists five basic sets of skills, or competencies, which can be systematically cultivated both at home and at school, that make up emotional intelligence.[18]

- Self-Awareness: Identifying your thoughts, feelings, and strengths, and recognizing how they influence choices and actions

- Social Awareness: Identifying and understanding the thoughts and feelings of others, developing empathy, and being able to take the perspective of others

- Self-Management: Handling emotions so that they facilitate rather than interfere with the task at hand; setting long- and short-term goals; and dealing with obstacles that may come your way

- Responsible Decision Making: Generating, implementing, and evaluating positive and informed solutions to problems, and considering the long-term consequences of your actions for yourself and others

- Relationship Skills: Saying no to negative peer pressure and working to resolve conflicts in order to maintain healthy and rewarding connections with individuals and groups

When social and emotional skills are taught and mastered, they help children succeed not just in school, but in all avenues of life. Numerous studies have found that young people who possess these social and emotional skills are in fact happier, more confident, and more capable as students, family members, friends, and workers.[19] At the same time, they are far less prone to drug or alcohol abuse, depression, or violence.

When parents and children practice and use the skills at home, the effects are doubly beneficial. Not only are young people better able to acquire the skills, but also relationships within the family tend to improve when family members listen to each other openly and solve problems together. Children also come to appreciate the fact that learning is a lifelong process, not something that stops when they leave school. Social and emotional learning is like an insurance policy for a healthy, positive, successful life.

CHAPTER 2

Preparing to Teach Children Exercises to Calm the Body and Focus the Mind

Now that you've chosen to go on this journey, you can feel supported knowing there are road maps to help you on your way. This chapter offers some guiding principles for cultivating children's inner strength, which will help children deepen their ability to quiet their minds and relax their bodies. We will explore the powerful role *you* play in encouraging your child to value stillness and quiet, and we will also teach skills in relaxing and paying attention through two techniques: (1) progressive muscle relaxation, and (2) mindfulness.

We suggest that you explore these skills first, so that you can derive for yourself the many benefits of these practices. More important, though, your own work will provide the necessary fertile ground for your child's growth and integration of these practices. Lastly, we'll provide you with details about how to use this guide, making it easy to get started and supporting both you and your child as the work grows and changes.

Learning a new way of being can be difficult for anyone, child and adult alike. But this journey may feel different than others you've been on, because it has no destination. The whole point is to have authentic, calming experiences with your child as you add to your repertoire of ways to deal with the stressful demands of your family's life.

Guiding Principle 1: Practice Stillness and Calming Techniques Yourself First before Trying Them with Your Child

We hope that you'll find that the new skills and techniques you are learning through this guide help you as much as they help your child. Before beginning this project with your child, try to set aside at least a couple of weeks to regularly practice the two contemplative techniques that you will be offering to teach your child. The stress-reduction benefits of both techniques—progressive muscle relaxation and mindfulness/present-moment awareness—require practice to be effective. And to authentically teach someone, it's helpful also to be a student of the techniques yourself.

When you practice these two contemplative techniques with the enclosed CD, use "Getting Relaxed: Ages 12 and Up," and "Paying Attention: Ages 12 and Up." It will be helpful to try each of these exercises yourself a couple of times before beginning to do them with your child. The first exercise will guide you through both a progressive muscle relaxation and a body scan; the second one consists of a mindfulness exercise. Since these exercises are excellent stress reducers, use them any time you feel stressed—or cultivate a regular habit of using them. For example, take a mindfulness break before starting your busy day, and later do a body scan before falling asleep.

Although this book is filled with creative ideas and suggestions for developing your child's inner strength, your *presence* is actually more important than the activities themselves. Your child will learn best through your example and modeling. Tobin Hart said it beautifully in his book *The Secret Spiritual World of Children*, when he wrote: "Mostly we teach by who we are and how we live. Our own development and that of our children are intertwined—we grow together." [1] It is important to be as committed to the development of your own inner life as you are to your child's inner life.

Guiding Principle 2: Your Role Is to Be a Co-learner and Guide

When children construct their own knowledge, they need a guide to help them, not an all-knowing authority. The best guides are genuinely learners themselves. When you help children nurture their inner lives, you expand your own inner pathways of knowing at the same time. It is a reciprocal relationship. Your role in this work, then, is simply to be willing to learn alongside your child and to help create a fertile ground for that learning.

Learning to ask open-ended questions rather than ones where there is an exact answer also helps you to stay in your role as co-learner. For example, an open-ended question would ask something like: What stood out for you in today's time together? A closed-ended question would ask: Tell me all the things we did together in our quiet time. Being fully present in the moment and listening deeply are also important elements of that process. While this requires some preparation on your part (which we cover in Guiding Principles 3 and 4), it relieves you from the responsibility of being the authority.

Sometimes your child may be the one teaching and leading you inward, if you allow that to happen. In fact, to most authentically do this work you simply need to (1) commit to integrating these practices and ways of being into the routines and rituals of your home; (2) commit to learning these practices yourself; (3) model these practices whenever possible; and (4) stay as open as your child already is to inner realms of knowing.

Guiding Principle 3: Children Learn Best by Actively Participating in Their Learning

When we went to school, many of us were exposed to a style of teaching that makes learning something the teacher does to the learner, rather than something you discover for yourself. In this type of learning, the teacher is the all-knowing authority, passing on information or directly teaching skills in a prescribed way; the child is simply the passive receiver of knowledge. But no doubt, as a parent, you have noticed how easily children can learn through play and other hands-on activities—often even without someone to facilitate that learning.

Tobin Hart calls play "the holy work of children" that helps them "find and define themselves."[2] When children construct their own knowledge through such hands-on play, what they learn is often more fully integrated into their lives, and becomes the building blocks for further learning and mastery. They are not passive participants in this model, but rather active agents of their learning, with their curiosity and confidence intact. They are not compelled to learn by an outside authority, but are led by their own curiosity and desire — imperatives of childhood that make children powerful learners, as well as teachers to those of us who spend our time with them.

Such a hands-on or "constructivist" approach is at the heart of this guide and the activities presented, which means that you'll want to cultivate a spirit of play, adventure, and genuine curiosity as you proceed. You are there to wait and see what unfolds. Try to let go of expectations that your child's learning should proceed in a certain way. For example, you won't be very successful in helping your children practice stillness and silence by simply telling them to calm down. They need direct, intuitive experiences in how calmness feels in their bodies and through their senses. They need to learn by experiencing it.

Guiding Principle 4: Allow Time for the Learning to Unfold

For both you and your child, learning to be more mindful and appreciative of silence is not likely to unfold in a straight line. There will be days when it might seem that nothing you're doing is working. Then suddenly, things will gel: when you lose your cool, your child might prompt you to take a breath, and you'll realize just how deeply she has been integrating these ideas. Gradually, what might feel at times forced or artificial about this work will become more automatic and authentic.

Try to commit to at least a couple of months of taking a regular quiet time together with your child so that the process has sufficient time to unfold. Check in periodically to ask your child how it's going and ask if there's anything she thinks you should change about what you are doing.

Guiding Principle 5: Integrate Rituals and New Routines into Your Family Life before Trying the Activities in the Guide and the CD

The practices you are about to introduce to your child offer both of you an opportunity for more quietness and stillness in your lives. Given the busy, sometimes frenzied nature of our lives, the contemplative moments are often missing. The more children can begin to experience moments of quiet and stillness, the more they will feel an inner balance and flow, which offsets the overstimulation that is so abundant in most of our lives.

Several weeks before doing the activities in the guide or on the CD, you can start to integrate some rituals and routines into your family life to expose your child to the opportunities that stillness and quiet can offer. Your goal with integrating these practices is to pique your child's curiosity, as well as to create readiness for her to learn the skills as they are presented in the guide and on the CD. It is important to wait for the right moments to introduce these new ways of being. By modeling these practices in your own interaction with your child and in how you structure your home, you are saying to your child that you value silence and stillness. You'll also be creating a more natural venue for changing deeply ingrained habits of how you respond to stressful events and for learning healthful ways that we hope will become lifelong habits. It's only through consistent practice that you will learn these skills.

The following rituals and routines can be thought of almost as a prerequisite for learning the specific exercises presented in Chapters 3, 4, and 5. Perhaps you can take a few minutes now to think through a typical day and, after reading the suggestions below, consciously commit to incorporating a few of the rituals and/or routines. Give thought to how each one might play out in practice in your home, and set yourself up for success by choosing those you know you can easily do daily or routinely. Throughout this book we mention various materials that enhance the use of these techniques. Some of these items may be hard to find, so we have provided a Materials Checklist at the end of the book with information about how to order them.

Have a Dinnertime Quieting Ritual

As part of a family ritual around dinnertime, a candle could be lit for a few moments of silence as everyone focuses on the flame of the candle. Focusing on an object can help the mind to move into a deeper state of calmness and clarity. Before you begin eating, you may each want to take a turn expressing one thing you are grateful for about the day.

Create a Peace Corner

A peace or calming corner is a special place that you set aside for members of your family. They can go there whenever they need calm and stillness, in order to regain their inner balance and flow. It could also be used when anyone is feeling overwhelmed, stressed, angry, or otherwise out of control emotionally—times when being alone would be helpful. Include your whole family in designing the space. You might include a picture or photo of a child's favorite peaceful place, elements from nature, calming pictures, quiet instrumental music, journals, chimes, mandala coloring books, etc. (see the Materials Checklist to order these items). Be sure the space is large enough for your child to lie down in, with comfortable pillows and a CD player with soothing music or recordings of sounds from nature. If you have young children, rather than a time-out, give your child a time-in: time to calm down in this corner.

Teach the "Keep Calm" Activity[3]

This simple, four-step breathing activity comes from the book *Emotionally Intelligent Parenting* by Maurice Elias, Steven Tobias, and Brian Friedlander. It can be used whenever your child is upset and self-control is needed. Teach these four simple steps to your child (and try it yourself!). Perhaps you might post these steps in your peace corner or other places in your home as a reminder.

1. Tell yourself, "Stop and take a look around."
2. Tell yourself, "Keep calm."
3. Take a deep breath through your nose while you count to five, hold it while you count to two, and then breathe out through your mouth while you count to five.
4. Repeat these steps until you feel calm.

Use Calming Music

Transitions and other stressful times during the day (such as when you're getting ready for school or trying to meet other pressures of time) are great times to stop for a moment and honor the shift from one activity to another. The sound of soft, slow classical music can really help change the way we feel at such moments. While you might use this music as background, it's even more effective if you take a "music break"—stop for even three minutes to listen quietly to a piece of music. This can be during times of transition, when your child is focusing on something intently and needs to stop, or if she starts to feel the symptoms of heightened stress. It is well known that listening to calming music has a direct correlation with a lowered respiration and heart rate, as well as changing our emotional mood.

Make Room for Silence and Stillness

One gift you can give yourself and your family is the gift of silence and stillness; it is simple to do, but rare in most of our homes. Try to find times in your day to take a quick break. Pause. Be still, be quiet, and take a few deep breaths together. Be present to the moment. For example, if you have a habit of turning on the radio for car rides, you can make it a family practice to have a few minutes of silence at the beginning and end of the car ride and ask children to notice what they see, hear, feel, etc., during that time. You can go on walks on your way to or from school or other errands and decide to be silent for some of the time. You can also decide to bring more moments of silence into an engaged activity, such as preparing food together or wrapping presents. Or, in your rare but precious one-on-one moments, simply be present to who your child truly is. These kinds of moments can actually help us keep in touch with our inner lives.

Address Violent or Disturbing Events Your Child Witnesses

If your child is unexpectedly exposed to something disturbing during the day—maybe she is watching television when a violent or frightening news story plays, or perhaps you've even come across a traffic accident or you see an ambulance rushing with sirens blaring—make it a practice to pause for a moment and send positive thoughts or healing to those in need. Rather than integrating the fear and stress reaction, your child will release much of the stress of the moment through having such a positive outlet.[4] Being able to talk about your child's concerns and being fully present as you listen to her questions are also crucial in how your child will remember and integrate any particular scary event.

Honor Nature and Provide Opportunities to Be Outdoors[5]

Nature provides important moments for stillness, as we connect to something larger than ourselves. Being in nature calls upon us to be in our bodies and reconnects the mind/body split. At the most basic level, out of doors there is room for children to run, shout, and play, releasing pent-up energy from their bodies accumulated through various stressors. We can breathe more deeply outdoors, simply because there is often more oxygen than indoors. And looking at a faraway horizon or sky can help us gain needed perspective on our small world, bounded by our bodies and lives. A relationship with nature is like any good relationship. It needs to unfold over time, moving toward intimacy and respect. We can perhaps then take on our challenges with a new, more optimistic attitude and cognitively restructure our attitudes about certain stresses. Sometimes all it takes is a new perspective to shift us out of the bad habits that keep us from being our best selves.

In addition to providing opportunities for your child to be in nature, help her to be present by engaging her senses. Your child will come to know whatever place she is outdoors through her body, not just her mind. Focusing on one sense at a time can be a very useful way to do this. Or simply notice changes in the season or in the night sky. You can help your child choose a peaceful place outdoors and then study that one place over time. For example, she could find a favorite tree near where you live and notice the changes that occur with it in each season of the year. The goal is for your child to develop a mindful presence outside—that is, one of being aware of her surroundings at a level of detail that transcends the relatively detached way we often experience nature.

Help Your Child Check into Her Body Cues

When children are younger, they often have the ability to tune in to their bodies' signals. As they grow older, they get messages from the outer world to turn off their natural sensitivity. However, before you can release stress, you need first to be aware that you *are* stressed. Help your child to learn the signs of stress through the checklist, "How Do I Feel When I Am Stressed?" in Chapter 4 (page 72). You can model this awareness yourself by making a note of times when your heart is beating fast, your breathing has become shallow, or you notice other signs of stress. You can also help your child to become more aware of her body's cues by using the biodots that are recommended in this book (see the Materials Checklist to order this item). These dots respond to the temperature of our bodies and through color changes tell us just how stressed (or calm) we are. Remember, it is equally important for you to notice your own stress triggers as well.

Use Story Time Effectively

Reading a story out loud together with your child can be a wonderful way to experience a contemplative moment—especially if it is done with intention. When reading a book, the pace immediately slows down, providing moments to pause along the way. You also experience each other's voice and can notice the various emotions that are stirring in both of you. There can be lots of unplanned moments where the story can take either of you to a deeper place. You might learn about a concern or deep question either of you has. Children also love the repetition of reading a book many times. The effects of this are quite similar to what we are cultivating in the contemplative practices you are about to teach your child. Repeating something—such as reading a book out loud, or listening to the CD that accompanies this book — helps strengthen a set of neural pathways in the brain that stores the memory for future use.

Now take a moment and list some of the ways you might be able to incorporate these rituals and routines into a typical day in the life of your family, using the form on the next page. For example:

Time of Day	Ritual or Routine
7:30 a.m.	Play some quiet music as children are getting ready for school

HOW THIS GUIDE IS ORGANIZED

Now you have paved the way for beginning this work by cultivating contemplative rituals and routines in your home and practicing the skills through the CD. Next, we recommend you take a closer look at Chapters 3, 4, and 5, which are organized by age. In these chapters you'll find activities you can do with your child for each of the two strategies for calming the body and focusing the mind: progressive muscle relaxation and mindfulness.

The CD tracks are also organized by age-level appropriateness. There are two exercises, entitled "Getting Relaxed" and "Paying Attention," for each of the following groups: ages five through seven, ages eight through eleven, and ages twelve and up. While the CD is the heart of this program, the activities we provide give you some ideas for what you can do with your child in preparation for the CD, and also after listening to the CD to help you and your child capture and integrate the learning. You may choose to do all of the activities or just some of them, based on what you know will work best for your child.

Throughout, we provide scripts to suggest how you might present the material to your child. These are only meant to provide you with a guide for what to say. Please feel free to adapt these scripts in any way that feels right and authentic for your relationship with your child.

MY RITUALS AND ROUTINES	
Time of Day	**Ritual or Routine**

Each calming exercise is followed by rituals and routines, called "Extensions into Daily Life," that are appropriate to the age level and draw on the lessons of the practice. Also featured is a section called "Story Time," which recommends age-appropriate stories to read with your child and includes suggestions for ways to discuss the books.

GETTING STARTED AND KEEPING IT GOING

Once you feel comfortable that you have integrated some rituals and routines into your family life and have consistently practiced the skills yourself, you can begin to do the exercises with your child.

The first time you do these activities with your child, you will want to use the guidebook along with the CD, following along with the activities as outlined for your child's age group. You'll start with the pre-CD activity, then listen to the CD track as recommended, and close with the post-CD activity. Here's a suggested process for getting prepared for that first time you sit down with your child with the guide and the CD:

1. *Read through the Activities:* Do a quick read of the recommended activities for the age of your child so that you understand the spirit and intent of each activity and can think through any adaptations you'd like to make. You may wish to read and listen to the CD tracks for the age levels below and/or above your child's in order to determine that you have the right fit. These are only suggested age levels.

   If you have more than one child and their ages are close, you may choose a track on the CD that you feel will work for both of them. If your children's ages are further apart, it may be more helpful to introduce the CD jointly and then have them listen to separate tracks using earphones. You may also decide to do these activities individually with each child in order to experience more quality time with each of them. Of course, depending on the number of children you have, this could be quite a commitment of time. However, it may be exactly what you and your children need to nurture a deeper level of communication with each other.

2. *Gather the Materials:* Take a look to see if there are any special materials you might need for an activity. Every activity needs the following:

   • Some sort of *bell or signal* to begin and end each activity. We recommend the Meinl Energy Chime, single chime — large size (see the Materials Checklist to order this item), but any bell can be used.

   • A *journal* for both you and your child. You can each make your own journals with a three-hole punch and some blank paper, binding it with yarn or string, or you can purchase notebooks or journals.

   Most of the other materials required are common household items that are relatively easy to find. Still, you should make sure to gather them before beginning the activity.

3. *Plan When:* Set aside a time and place to begin when you think you can create a sense of calm and focus. It's helpful to keep to a certain time of day so that it becomes easier and easier to fit it into your schedule.

4. *Do the Two Exercises for Your Child's Age at Different Times:* We don't recommend that you do the two activities one right after the other. Be sure to leave some time in between the two exercises as outlined for your child's age: "Getting Relaxed" and "Paying Attention." You may decide to do the first exercise (progressive muscle relaxation) and practice it several times before you go to the second exercise, on mindfulness.

5. *Plan for Ongoing Practice:* Together with your child, it would be ideal to commit to using either one of the CD tracks — "Getting Relaxed" or "Paying Attention" — at least three times a week. After the first introduction to each particular exercise, you'll no longer do the pre-CD activities in the guide. From that time on, you'll only use the CD track, take time for reflection in your journals, and perhaps try out some of the extension activities. There

may be some extension activities for other age groups that could work for you as well.

6. *Continue and Add to the Rituals and Routines:* All along you'll be continuing the rituals and routines you chose to start two to three weeks before beginning with the CD. As you get more comfortable with the activities, you might want to add some additional rituals and routines (we provide a list in the "extensions" section of each activity), or feel free to create your own!

BACKGROUND INFORMATION ABOUT THE TWO STRATEGIES: GETTING RELAXED AND PAYING ATTENTION

In the first session, children are introduced to some of the concepts and skills that help them understand how stress affects the quality of our lives. Stress is the body's reaction to any situation that we perceive as an emergency. It is not the events or circumstances themselves. It is our bodies' reaction to them.

Stress is registered in the body as a danger reaction known as the "fight, flight, or freeze" response, which is an innate, automatic response. This response causes a certain set of physiological reactions in the body: our heart rate increases, blood is distributed to the muscles for strength, our pupils dilate, and digestion shuts down. The problem is that in modern life we overuse the "fight, flight, or freeze" response, because we respond to many situations as if they are life-threatening when they are not. As a result, our nervous systems don't have time to recover, because we are activating this response too frequently. When stress is chronic, it is difficult for the body to cope. As a result, stress overload can lead to stress-related illness.

Fortunately, in the late 1960s, researchers at Harvard University, including Herbert Benson, noticed the existence of a counterbalancing mechanism to the "flight, fight, or freeze" response. It consisted of a similarly coordinated set of physiological responses. Benson named this the "relaxation response." The relaxation response can be triggered by simply sitting quietly and focusing the body on relaxation through meditation, visualization, quiet movement, art and music, or by intentionally and systematically relaxing muscles. The researchers found that although the stress response was involuntary, the relaxation response required practice. [6]

The calming strategies in this book offer children two different tools to manage their stress effectively by triggering the relaxation response. First, it is important to focus on deep breathing as a key ingredient in any calming activity. Breathing deeply and regularly is one of the quickest and most accessible ways to increase relaxation and awareness while releasing tension and stress. However, only abdominal breathing (also known as diaphragmatic breathing) helps release deep stress.

It is also important to become more aware of what some of our stressors are and notice how our bodies react. At first we may not necessarily be aware of how much stress we hold in our bodies, even though our bodies register stress before we are consciously aware of it. Tension in our muscles is the body's signal that we are under stress.

ABOUT GETTING RELAXED

In the first calming strategy, "Getting Relaxed," we help children learn how to be internally aware of how much tension they are experiencing in their bodies and how to progressively relax their muscles. Progressive muscle relaxation comes from the work of a physician, Edmund Jacobson, who published the book *Progressive Relaxation* in 1938. The premise is based on the idea that the muscles in the body register anxiety-provoking thoughts and events. A build-up of muscle tension then increases the actual feelings of anxiety. Dr. Jacobson proposed that the opposite is true as well: if muscles relax, then physiological tension is reduced, and in turn anxiety is reduced. The progressive relaxation technique consists of tensing and relaxing major muscle groups while paying attention to the sensations in each part of the body. There are ten major muscle groups, and it is best when each muscle group is squeezed and relaxed twice before moving to the next area of the body.[7] It is also important to tense each muscle group before the relaxing phase, which should last twice as long as the tensing phase. Jacobson's original work shows that tightening a muscle and then relaxing it helps to relax that part of the body even more deeply.[8]

The physiological benefits of progressive muscle relaxation include reduction of pulse rate, blood pressure, and respiratory rate. This strategy can be very effective in counteracting anxiety when it arises in the body. Once an individual is taught the basic sequence of tightening and relaxing the muscle groups, this can be used along with body scanning.

Body scanning also focuses on body awareness and helps one tune in to areas of tension in the body. An individual, either alone or led by someone, closes his eyes and begins by bringing attention to his toes, slowly working up the body by bringing attention to its different parts. He inwardly asks himself whether he is feeling any tension or discomfort in that part of his body, and uses awareness to relax the area of tension.

Both these strategies help us notice where we store muscle tension. We can then be more in control of letting it go. Chronic muscle tension restricts digestion and decreases energy. When we increase our awareness of our bodies' cues, we can practice this strategy when we need to, resulting in a gradual decrease in the amount of tension we hold in the body.

ABOUT "PAYING ATTENTION"

In the second calming exercise presented in this book, "Paying Attention," we help children experience mindfulness as a way of improving their ability to pay attention to the present moment without judgment. It is a capacity that everyone has, and it can be nurtured through practice and integrated into everyday life. Mindfulness as a calming tool teaches us to bring our full attention to what we are doing, when we are doing it. Mindfulness can be practiced as a kind of meditation or used as a way of bringing our full attention to everyday activities, such as taking a walk or preparing a meal.

During a mindfulness exercise that is done while being still, we welcome wherever the mind goes by simply noting and labeling where our thoughts have drifted and then returning our attention to our breath as an anchor. It is useful to label thoughts that come and go, using simple words like "hearing," "thinking," and "feeling." The process of doing that helps us notice where our attention is so that we can then bring ourselves back to our breath. The main task of mindfulness awareness is to strengthen our ability to pay attention. We do not judge ourselves when our minds wander, since it's only natural. We simply return to our breath as the anchor of our experience. We strengthen mindfulness in the same way we strengthen other habits—through practice!

Research has shown mindfulness meditation practice and its integration into daily life to be a stress reducer, an immune system enhancer, and an effective calming strategy.[9] But most important, mindfulness cultivates a sense of serenity, slowing down the racing thoughts set off by our daily stressors and providing us with the energy and coping strategies we need to face our challenges. When we are mindful, we are wholehearted about our experience. We are doing one thing at a time, focused and aware of that one thing, and entering that thing completely. This reengages us with the world around us and with ourselves. Mindfulness can be practiced in stillness and as a habit of awareness to cultivate during regular daily life. That is, we can approach any daily task—such as brushing our teeth, dressing, and eating—with the type of full attention and wholeheartedness cultivated in mindfulness. In fact, it is helpful with children to start by doing mindfulness experiences in their daily life before going to a mindfulness exercise that requires them to be still.

CHAPTER 3

Exercises to Calm the Body and Focus the Mind for Five- to Seven-Year-Olds

DEVELOPMENTAL ISSUES AFFECTING FIVE- TO SEVEN-YEAR-OLDS

Children ages five through seven have natural curiosity, wonder, and joy about the world around them. As a result, they will probably respond positively — with interest and openness — to the idea of learning new things about quieting the mind and relaxing the body. Likewise, they welcome "alone time" with their parents and enjoy participating in common activities together. This special kind of quiet time can serve to help children express their feelings and thoughts as well as provide a sense of warmth and safety. Having a regular time to check in with you helps the five- to seven-year-old child begin to voice concerns or deep questions that need a more relaxed atmosphere to be expressed.

Although children this age may not yet easily verbalize their understanding of consciousness, it is now clearer that young children do have the ability to separate out thoughts in the mind from people and things outside of themselves.[1] Since children's skills in this area are emerging, your child may or may not be able to understand the theory of why she is doing this work, but will respond to the concrete practices, images, and play that these activities present, especially when practices are made regular as rituals and routines. For example, your child may not be able to apply these practices when she is.upset by you simply saying something like, "You need to calm down." But if you say instead, "Would you like to take a break and listen to the calming CD or do some deep breathing with your breathing buddy?" over many times of using that ritual, the child will start to relate its benefits to herself and perhaps even suggest herself that she needs to take a break with her breathing buddy when she's feeling upset.

A young child's brain changes physiologically as a result of environmental experiences. Neural connections (synapses) are forming rapidly at this age, and enriched opportunities such as the ones provided in this book and CD have a very positive effect on brain development.

WHAT TO REMEMBER ABOUT THIS AGE GROUP

- Children this age are able to find the words to bring what they are thinking and feeling into their awareness by being given the opportunity to verbalize them. Also, children of this age have a new level of self-awareness that makes them able to make evaluative judgments about themselves.

- Parental approval and identification — wanting to be like the important adults in their lives — is critical for children at this stage of development. They develop positive self-esteem by being able to accomplish new things and being competent at them. Since they are not happy with failure, it is important to approach learning these new skills slowly so that they meet both with success and with your support and encouragement.

- One of the ways five- to seven-year-olds begin to develop coping strategies for dealing with stressful situations is through play — pretending to do some things they may not yet have the skills for. Adults can assume an active role in helping structure a healthy play opportunity — one that is exploratory in nature — such as the ones we provide on this CD. It's important to keep a spirit of "there's no right answer" during this type of play. You are exploring alongside your child, and any reactions or insights or inclinations that come up during these experiences should be validated.

- Children welcome explicit instructions when learning something new, as long as parental assurance and encouragement are present. Young children's minds are curious and imaginative, so concrete and imaginative thinking can go hand in hand.

- At this stage of development, children are able to concentrate on quiet activities for about twenty minutes, so varying their experience with the material presented is essential. The process is more important than the outcome or product, although five- to seven-year-olds are starting to be able to sense the concept of cause and effect. For example, the idea that stress has certain effects in the body is something that they can begin to grasp.

- A child of this age likes routines and rituals. Repetitive behavior maximizes a five- to seven-year-old's learning. Making these practices a regular part of your and your child's daily life will be welcomed.

- At the heart of this experience is your relationship with your child. Enjoy the journey!

☼ EXERCISE

GETTING RELAXED: PROGRESSIVE MUSCLE RELAXATION

This exercise is Track 1 on the CD.

In this session children will be introduced to the idea of having a regular quiet time together with you to help calm their minds and relax their bodies. They will contrast how they feel in a relaxed state and in a stressful one. They will learn two techniques for releasing tension stored in their bodies: deep belly breathing and progressive muscle relaxation. You'll help your child practice belly breathing through a "breathing buddy" — a soft toy that can be placed on her belly. After a guided experience on the CD of tensing and releasing various muscles, you'll introduce "reflection journals" — a place where both of you can regularly explore your feelings about the experience through art, writing, or other musings.

○○○ **BEFORE LISTENING TO THE CD**

What You'll Need

☐ Bell/chime (optional — see the Materials Checklist to order this item)

☐ Stuffed animal or small soft toy (about the size of a child's fist)

☐ The book *Building Emotional Intelligence*

☐ A CD player and the CD *Building Emotional Intelligence* cued up to "Getting Relaxed: Ages 5–7"

☐ Two journals: one for you and one for your child (you can use paper, pens, crayons, and/or color markers and yarn or ribbon to make your own books, or buy notebooks with blank pages)

☐ A peaceful time and place to sit with your child, large enough to lie down comfortably

Time You'll Need: 30 Minutes

Concepts and Skills

Children will:

• contrast how their bodies feel when they are calm versus when they are stressed

• practice using deep belly breathing to relax their bodies

• experience relaxing their bodies through progressively tensing and releasing different muscles

What to Remember

• One of the best and most accessible ways to release tension and built-up stress is through deep belly breathing.

• In order to let go of tension through progressively tensing and releasing muscles, it is important to hold the tension in each area of the body for a few seconds and then let go of the contracted muscle quickly, rather than gradually.

Setting the Stage

• Begin by introducing your child to the new things you will be learning together through working with this book and CD. You might say something like:

We're going to be taking some special quiet time together, perhaps a couple of times a week. And during this time, we're going to practice some things we can do whenever we feel the need to relax our bodies and calm down.

• Mention to your child that you would like to always begin this special time together with a little silence and that you will ring a chime once and ask her to listen to the sound of the chime until she hears it has stopped ringing and to raise her hand when she can no longer hear the chime. Be patient with your child, especially if silence is something unusual for her. It may take time for her to adjust to the possibilities silence provides.

• Explain that you're going to help her notice what her body feels like when she is worried or upset about something and then notice how different her body feels when she is calm again. The following activity is rooted in creative play, which is how children of this age begin to make sense of their world. You might start by saying:

Let's go on a little imaginary journey and pretend we're climbing to the top of a big mountain . . . Let's stand up and put on our hiking boots and climbing gloves [pause and put on imaginary boots and gloves] *OK, here we go . . . Follow me!* [Begin to slowly walk around the room.]

Oh, oh! We just walked into a giant mud puddle . . . the mud is really deep . . . we're sinking in up to our ankles . . . each step is hard to take . . . it feels like your feet might be getting stuck . . . you can barely pull each foot out . . . Try reaching up and pulling on one of these tree branches above us . . . like this. [Model reaching up, pulling with tight-fisted grip.] *Keep going . . . Phew! We made it across. Let's sit down and take a break.*

- Together explore how that felt:

  How are your legs feeling after walking through that mud?

  What about your arms when you were grasping the tree branches and pulling yourself up?

  Did you notice anything about how you were breathing or how your heart was beating? Let's feel our chests right now.

  Sometimes, we can notice changes in our bodies when we get upset, worried, or when we've been working really hard . . . Our hands may feel different; they might get cold and damp . . . Maybe our hearts beat faster . . . Even our breathing can change. We might notice ourselves taking quick little breaths or even holding our breath . . .

  Explore any other sensations in your body either of you noticed.

- Now let her explore how her body feels when it is calm:

  I would like us to imagine where we just were. So let's start walking again. [Begin to walk slowly and stop.] *Let's imagine, as we are walking, that we come to a beach on a warm summer afternoon. Let's lie down and get comfortable and feel the cool sand on our backs.* [Lie down.] *See if you can hear the ocean waves, one after the next . . . Feel yourself relaxing into the sand . . . Just enjoy resting your body here for a few moments . . .* [Pause for about ten seconds.] *Great . . . Now gently sit up and ask yourself: How do my legs feel now? How about my arms and hands? How about my breath and heartbeat?*

  Our hands might feel warm. Maybe our breathing became slower and deeper. Did our legs and arms feel relaxed? Our heartbeat might have slowed down.

  Explore any other sensations in your bodies either of you noticed.

- Mention that this special quiet time together can help us learn some ways we can calm down when we need to.

Introduce Belly Breathing

- Explain to your child that being aware of the way we breathe is a very important part of learning how to quiet the mind and relax the body when we feel upset:

  One of the ways we can relax is by breathing really deeply.

- Ask your child to lie comfortably on the floor and begin to pay attention to her breathing, and notice where she feels the air going in and out. Place a small soft toy (about the size of a small fist) on your child's belly, so she can see what part of her body is rising when she breathes in. You can introduce the toy as her breathing buddy. One of the ways we know we're taking a deep breath is when we see our bellies going up and down, rather than just our chests. You might say:

  Take in a breath and notice where your breath is going. Is your chest going up? Is any other part of your body rising? Now let it out. What part of your body is moving?

  When we take a really deep breath, not only our chests go up, but our bellies do, too. Let's try and see if we can bring the air all the way down to our bellies by watching the soft toy. See if you can make it go up when we breathe in and down when we breathe out.

  Breathe in to a count of 4: 1, 2, 3, 4.

  Breathe out: 1, 2, 3, 4.

  Repeat a few more times until she has made her toy rise on her belly on the in breath and it goes down on the out breath. If the child is still not bringing her breath all the way down to her belly, you can gently put your hand on the soft toy to help.

- Explain that the more air we breathe in, the better it is for our bodies. The same is true for the air we breathe out. It is good for our bodies to breathe deeply, taking in as much air as we can and letting out as much air as we can. That helps our bodies work better. It is like giving our bodies the food we need to stay healthy.

◎ ◎ ◎ **LISTENING TO THE CD**

(Have the CD ready, cued to "Getting Relaxed: Ages 5–7" for the next part of the activity.)

- Now have your child gently sit up. Introduce the idea that you will now be listening to a CD together that will guide you both through an experience of relaxing your bodies. Explain that the person's voice on the CD is a man named Daniel Goleman. You might say:

    So, one of the things we're going to be doing each time we have this special time together is also to listen to a CD by a man named Daniel Goleman, who knows a lot about how to help people calm themselves. He is going to say some things that will help us relax all of the parts of our bodies.

    You'll notice that your body is going to relax and your mind is going to focus on a few things. You'll notice it might make you feel calmer. What we are learning today can also be used some other time when we are feeling upset or scared. The more we practice this, the easier it gets to become calmer or more relaxed when we need to. Are you ready? I am going to do this with you, too.

    Let's lie down again on the floor. The CD is going to tell us to slowly notice different parts of our bodies. We're going to first tense that part up real tightly and hold it for a while, and then we're going to quickly let that part of our bodies go.

    You might want to show the child what you mean by clenching a fist and counting to five, then relaxing it and counting to ten.

- Settle comfortably on the floor with your child's breathing buddy close by.

- Start the CD.

Getting Relaxed: Progressive Muscle Relaxation (CD Script)

For five- to seven-year-olds: 6:06 minutes

Welcome to this special quiet time together. We're going to learn how to relax ourselves and notice how different parts of our bodies feel when we're relaxed: our heads, our shoulders, our arms and hands, our bellies, our legs — all the way down to the tips of our toes.

Let's lie down comfortably on the floor, on your back with your arms at your sides, and place your breathing buddy — that can be any soft toy the size of your fist — place your breathing buddy on your belly to help remind you to breathe so your belly gets bigger.

Take a little stretch or wiggle if you need to and get really comfortable. Let yourself begin to get really relaxed . . . and now close your eyes.

Now take a big belly breath and feel your belly getting big like a balloon. Breathe in . . . in . . . in . . . in . . . And now slowly let the air out: 1, 2, 3, 4.

And take another belly breath in and feel your belly getting bigger and your breathing buddy rising: 1, 2, 3, 4 . . . and out: 1, 2, 3, 4.

Now imagine you have a ball of clay in each hand . . . Squeeze the clay with your hands . . . Make your fists tight . . . Squeeze . . . squeeze . . . squeeze . . . as tightly as you can. And now let go . . . Let the clay just drop to the floor . . . Feel your arms relaxing . . . Let your hands relax . . . Let your fingers relax . . . Let your arms relax . . . completely . . . while I count to 5: 1, 2, 3, 4 . . . 5.

Good . . . Your hands and arms are relaxed.

Now lift your shoulders up toward your ears . . . Keep squeezing them up there . . . as tightly as you can . . . Keep squeezing them up a little more . . . Now let go and let your shoulders relax . . . Let them drop back down . . . Let your shoulders relax completely . . . while I count to 5: 1, 2, 3, 4, 5 . . . . Great . . . Your shoulders are relaxed.

Now squeeze your eyes tight . . . Squint like you do when the sunlight is too bright . . . Open your mouth as wide as you can . . . like you're going to take a giant bite, and stick out your tongue . . . Hold . . . hold . . . hold . . . Now let go and let your whole face relax . . . Let your face relax and rest while I count to 5: 1, 2, 3, 4 . . . 5. Your face is relaxed.

Now try to pull in your belly as much as you can toward your back . . . and give yourself a great big hug . . . Keep hugging the whole middle of your body as tightly as you can . . . Hug . . . hug . . . hug . . . Now relax . . . Let your belly be soft . . . Let your chest relax and let your arms fall to the floor as I count to 5: 1, 2, 3, 4, 5 . . . Good . . . Your belly and chest are relaxed.

Now tighten your legs and feet, making them stiff, and curl all ten toes ... Keep holding your legs and squeezing ... And now let go and relax ... Feel your legs and feet resting on the floor ... as I count to 5: 1, 2, 3, 4, 5. Your feet and legs are relaxed.

And now one last time ... tighten up your whole body ... Tighten your hands ... arms ... shoulders ... face ... belly ... chest ... legs ... feet ... Tighten everything and make your body as stiff as you can ... And now ... let go. Let your whole body relax as you lie down and feel like you are melting into the floor.

Take a belly breath in ... and let it out ... Again, in ... and out ... One more time on your own ... You can hear your breath relaxing you.

Now take a little time to notice if any part of your body might still feel tight or uncomfortable ... Check in with your body and ask yourself ... are my feet relaxed? Do my legs feel relaxed? How do my arms feel? Take a little time to see how your whole body is feeling ... from your toes all the way to the top of your head. Notice how your body is feeling right now.

Now gently open your eyes and begin to wiggle your toes and your fingers and let your body take a stretch and slowly begin to sit up and feel how relaxed your body feels. That's wonderful. You just learned how to help your body feel calm and relaxed — and you can do this again anytime you want.

Thanks for trying this out with me.

What to Do

- Help your child explore and reflect on what happened during the progressive muscle relaxation:

    How are you feeling right now? How are your arms feeling? Your legs? Let's feel our breath by putting our hands on our chests and bellies. How does that feel? What parts of your body were easy to relax? Hard to relax?

- Introduce the reflection journal as a tool for regular drawing and writing, as a way to reflect during these quiet times together. You might say:

    One of the ways we can remember what we did today is to draw or write in a journal about our experience together. This way, each time we do this activity, we can keep track of what happened when we tried these things out. We can decorate our journals any way we want. For today, I thought we could perhaps draw a picture of our bodies relaxed. Think about some colors that remind you of feeling calm and peaceful. What are the colors you are thinking of?

    You might choose to draw to calming, soft music.

- When you both are finished, have your child share her drawing, and invite her to comment on anything she wants to. Feel free to share yours as well.

- Mention that you will try to spend this special time together a couple of times a week and maybe even more often later:

    Each time we sit down to do this, we'll do an activity together first. We might draw, or read a story, or pretend to act out something. Then we'll listen to the CD. Afterward we'll talk about what happened and draw or write in our journals.

- End by explaining that you will close this special time together the same way that you started—by ringing a bell to signal the start of a moment of silence. Ask your child to raise her hand when she no longer hears the bell.

- Ring the bell.

Extensions into Daily Life

- Refer to Guiding Principle 5: Integrate Rituals and New Routines (Chapter 2) for ways to continue to incorporate and reinforce the exercises learned. For example, your peace corner might now include the CD *Building Emotional Intelligence,* so your children can use it on their own whenever they need some quiet time.

- Before bed is a great time to practice breathing exercises as a way of letting go of the stresses of the day. Lying close to your child, you can also synchronize your breathing to hers and quietly name whatever tensions from the day you are letting go. Or practice abdominal breathing as your child "blows out the lights" for the day before you leave the room. Simply ask your child to place the soft toy on her belly and breathe in deeply to a count of four. As she breathes out to a count of four, have her direct all her air toward the light switch. Turn off the light when she has exhaled all the air.

- Use deep abdominal breathing or progressive muscle relaxation as a way to help your child calm down when she or you notice she is upset or angry. Ask her if she could take some deep breaths and/or practice tensing parts of the body and letting them go.

Story Time

When you have story time with your child, you might together read the book *There's a Big, Beautiful World Out There!* by Nancy Carlson. In this book, the author writes, "There's a lot to be scared of, for sure," as she takes children on a journey through some of children's common fears. Yet "if you hide under your covers," you'll miss a lot of what's beautiful about our world, too.

You might begin by saying:

Let's see what the children in this book sometimes get upset about and see if they are the kinds of things that upset you, too.

Read the book. You might occasionally interject whether that is something your child has experienced or has become upset by.

After reading, discuss:

What were some things that the children in the book were thinking would scare them? Do any of those things scare you? What else does? What happens to your body when you feel scared? [Remind your child of some of the things you spoke about during quiet time.]

What did the children in the story want to do because they were scared? If they hid under their covers, what are some things they would miss out on? Have you ever not done something because you felt it would be too hard or would make you scared? What are some things we learned in quiet time together that we could do that may help us in a situation like this?

Another good book to read aloud is *The Wonderful Happens* by Cynthia Rylant. This book describes how "the world is filled with so many wonderful things — birds that fly though the sky, cats napping in windows . . . and then there's the most wonderful thing of all — you!" After reading the book together, you can explore what your child feels makes her wonderful — her unique gifts, talents, and ways of being. It is also an opportunity to say what you feel is special about her. Finally, the book provides a wonderful opportunity to "find" the different things that are wonderful, thanks to the beautiful illustrations of Coco Dowley.

EXERCISE

PAYING ATTENTION: MINDFULNESS

This exercise is Track 2 on the CD.

In this session, children will be introduced to the practice of mindfulness, which quiets the mind and focuses the attention using the breath as a focus point. Mindfulness is a way of paying attention to the present moment without judgment. Children will bring their full attention to simple everyday activities such as looking and really seeing their surroundings through a game of I-Spy, slowly and deliberately eating a raisin, and carefully listening to the sounds around them through a guided experience of mindfulness on the CD. You'll also give your child a chance to be mindful using the sense of touch in a mystery box activity, and generally explore ways to build mindfulness into his everyday life.

○○○ **BEFORE LISTENING TO THE CD**

What You'll Need

☐ Bell/chime

☐ Four or five common objects — which you will use in a game of I-Spy — placed around the area where you are doing this session (you can use any item as long as you can describe it in such a way that your child will understand what it is)

☐ Two raisins for each person, with paper plates and napkins (if your child can't or won't eat raisins, use blueberries or grapes)

☐ A "mystery box" — a shoe box or any other box with an hole cut in it large enough for a hand to fit through, but not large enough to see the objects within (place a few items in the box that are interesting to touch, such as a peeled grape, a button, a shoelace, a cotton ball, a sponge, a small rubber ball, a cucumber slice, etc.)

☐ Two reflection journals, and pens, crayons, or colored markers

☐ The book *Building Emotional Intelligence*

☐ A CD player and the CD *Building Emotional Intelligence* cued up to "Paying Attention: Ages 5–7"

Time You'll Need: 30 Minutes

Concepts and Skills

Children will:

• articulate the meaning of "mindfulness" as being aware of what's happening as it's happening

• practice quieting the mind by using the breath as an anchor

• learn how to bring attention to moment-to-moment awareness using different senses

What to Remember

• The thoughts, feelings, and sensations that come up during a mindfulness activity are not considered distractions. They are welcomed without judgment and become part of the experience.

- Children can learn to think of their breath as an anchor. While the mind may drift like a boat, they can always return to the awareness of their breath as a way of bringing their attention to the present moment.

- During an experience of mindfulness, it is useful to label thoughts that come and go, using simple words like "hearing," "thinking," and "feeling." The process of labeling helps children to notice where their attention is, so they can then bring themselves back to their breath.

- Mindfulness can be practiced as a form of meditation and as a habit of awareness to cultivate during regular daily life. That is, we can approach any daily task—such as brushing our teeth, dressing, and eating—with the kind of full attention and wholeheartedness cultivated in mindfulness.

Setting the Stage

- Remind your child that you would like to begin each session with a moment of silence. Explain that you will ring the bell once. Ask your child to raise his hand when he doesn't hear the bell anymore. Ring the bell.

- You'll begin to expose the child to the concept of mindfulness through "mindful seeing." Explain that this next exercise will help your child quiet his mind, and that when we are calm, we are able to focus better and pay attention when we need to. You might introduce this session this way:

  Remember when we had our last special quiet time together and we practiced relaxing our bodies? What was your favorite part about what we did last time? Today we are going to do some things that quiet our minds and help us pay attention better. We are going to practice something called "mindfulness." It sounds like a big word, but what it means is to be able to know what you are feeling or thinking right now and paying attention to what you are doing as you are doing it.

A Game of I-Spy

• Introduce a game of I-Spy, which is a guessing game where you describe something you see in the general vicinity and the child tries to guess what it is you are looking at.

    Let's try a game called I-Spy. Have you ever played it before? It's a way to start noticing what it is like to see mindfully. In I-Spy I'll tell you about something I see or "spy with my little eye," and you'll try to guess what it is. I'll start.

• Begin with an example. Pick an object such as a toy ball in the room in plain sight of your child and describe it:

    I spy with my little eye . . . something round and blue.

    Add more description if your child needs it, e.g., "It's about as big as your fist; it bounces," etc., until he guesses what you are looking at.

• Explain that the object of this game is not to win or lose, but to notice what is in the room and really, really look closely at everything around us. Try a few rounds of I-Spy, with you first describing the object and your child guessing. Then have the child describe an object, and you guess what it is.

• Ask your child what he thought of the game of I-Spy:

    How was that game for you? Did you notice anything in the room that you hadn't noticed before? What?

• Explain that what you were doing in this game was seeing mindfully.

Mindfully Eating a Raisin

• Now explain that you will do something else that you do every day—just like seeing. You will *eat* something in a mindful way. Give your child and yourself two raisins each on a paper plate or napkin.

• You might want to give your child a chance to eat one raisin before continuing. You could say:

    I've got these raisins. I'm wondering if you'd like to taste one before we begin this activity.

• Now ask your child to bring all of his attention to the second raisin.

Ask him to take a few moments now to look very carefully at his raisin and then pick it up (but explain that he is not to put it in his mouth yet). Ask him for words that describe the raisin:

What are some words to describe your raisin? What color is it? How big is it? Is it soft or hard? What else do you notice about it?

- Have your child pick up the raisin and eventually put it into his mouth and eat it. You could say:

So, in a moment, we are each going to put a raisin in our mouths. We are going to let the raisins stay in our mouths without biting them yet, until I put up my fingers from 1 to 5. Just feel the raisin with your tongue. Ready? 1, 2, 3, 4, 5. Now slowly begin to chew it as I count to 5 again. Don't swallow it yet. Think to yourself, "How does it taste?" Wait until I count to 5: 1, 2, 3, 4, 5, and now swallow it.

As you're eating your raisin as well, just put up your fingers from 1 to 5.

- Ask:

So what was that like? What happened? What did you notice? Was that hard or easy to do? Why?

Share your own insights.

○○○ **LISTENING TO THE CD**

(Have the CD ready, cued to "Paying Attention: Ages 5–7," for the next part of the activity.)

- Introduce the "Paying Attention: Mindfulness" exercise, an experience your child will be led through by Daniel Goleman.

   So far we've used our eyes to really look and pay attention to the things around us through I-Spy. And then we used our mouths to really taste our food by paying close attention to eating. Now for the second time, we'll be listening to the CD where the man named Daniel Goleman will be leading us through another experience of quieting our minds and relaxing our bodies. For this one, we'll have to put on our listening ears to see what we notice when we really pay attention to what we hear. Are you ready? We need to be sitting in our chairs with our feet on the ground and our hands on our legs. And remember, he is going to remind us to breathe really deeply into our bellies. Let's begin.

- Start the CD.

Paying Attention: Mindfulness (CD Script)

For five- to seven-year-olds: 7:03 minutes

Let's have some special quiet time together. We're going to spend some time noticing what's happening each moment — especially noticing some sounds. Let's begin by sitting comfortably in your chair . . . with your feet on the floor . . . your hands resting in your lap . . . and your head held high, like it's being lifted gently by a balloon floating above you. Ready? Take a deep breath so the air goes into your belly . . . Breathe in 1, 2, 3, 4 . . . and slowly breathe out 1, 2, 3, 4 . . . And again breathe in 1, 2, 3, 4 . . . and out . . . 1, 2, 3, 4. Good.

Now, gently close your eyes and take another deep belly breath in . . . and let it gently out . . . Now listen to my voice as we take an imaginary journey. We're going to practice being mindful by bringing all of our attention to what we are hearing.

So let's begin by listening to the sound of the bell and noticing how long you can hear it ring . . .

[The sound of a chime.]

And now take another breath in . . . and out . . . in . . . and out . . .

As you sit quietly, you may hear some other sounds as well. When you hear a new sound, just name it silently to yourself. Tell yourself what you think you are hearing. Let's start by taking a breath in . . . and out . . . in . . . and out . . .

[Silence. The sound of a bird chirping. Silence.]

When you hear the sound, just name it . . . [The sound of a bird chirping. Silence.]

Say to yourself very quietly, "Bird" . . . and if you hear the same sound again just say to yourself, "Bird . . . bird . . . "

[The sound of a bird chirping. Silence. The bird chirps again. Silence. The bird chirps again.]

And notice your breath going in . . . and out . . . in . . . and out . . . I think we are ready to practice listening mindfully to some more sounds. Remember, while you are waiting to hear something, keep breathing in . . . and out. And when you hear a sound, just name it to yourself if you think you know what it is.

[Silence. The sound of water dripping very slowly.]

Remember to name the sound "water" each time you hear it.

[Silence. The sound of water dripping very slowly.]

And breathe in . . . and out . . . in . . . and out. . . . And listen for a few more sounds before we end . . . Remember to say to yourself what you think the sound is.

[The sound of a drum beating slowly four times.]

[Long silence. The sound of a cat meowing. Silence. Meow. Silence. Meow. Silence. Meow. Silence.]

Let's close by listening mindfully to the bell one last time.

[Silence. The sound of the chime.]

Thanks for trying this out with me.

○○○ **AFTER LISTENING TO THE CD**

What to Do

- Help your child explore and reflect on what happened during the mindfulness exercise:

    What are some of the sounds you heard? Was it easy or hard to guess what the sound was? Did it feel like a short time? A long time? How do you feel right now?

    Summarize any comments or insights.

Play a Mystery Box Game

- Introduce a "mystery box" game. Have available a mystery box, packed with everyday objects that are interesting to touch, as described under "What You'll Need" above.

    Now that we've had a chance to pay attention by looking, tasting, and listening, let's use our hands and explore what it feels like to really pay attention and be mindful when we touch things. We'll play a "mystery box" game.

- Show your child the mystery box and let him hold it if he'd like.

- In this game, the child will close his eyes and put his hands into the box, touching one object at a time. He can touch that object and try to describe what he is touching until he thinks he is ready to guess what it might be. Give your child a few minutes to just describe what he is touching before he makes a guess at the object's identity. After a minute or two of describing what he is touching, prompt him:

    Are you ready to guess what you are touching? Let's take it out of the box.

- Remind your child that, as in the I-Spy game, the object of this game is not to win or lose, but simply to pay close attention to what something feels like. So while it might be fun to guess the correct object, it's also interesting to see what other ideas come up for the child based on what he is feeling.

- Give your child a few chances to touch, describe, and then guess an object and then take it out of the box. Ask:

  How were you able to guess what something was? How was it to touch something without knowing what it was? How did that feel to you? Were you surprised by anything in this game?

- Now pull out your reflection journals and remind your child how your special journal is one way that you can remember what you've learned during your time together.

  Just like we really pay attention when we look, taste, listen, or touch objects, we can put all of our attention to anything we do, any time we do it. So when we color or draw we can pay close attention to what we are doing. Let's draw something from today's session in our reflection journals — it might be what we tasted, or an object we looked at, or something we touched or even heard on the CD. As you draw the different things, notice whether you used your eyes or ears, taste, or touch to learn about them.

- Discuss a few ways that we might be able to be mindful — or really pay close attention — to something we do all the time in our lives. You might ask the child to think of something he is going to do before he goes to sleep tonight that he could do mindfully, e.g., brush his teeth. Ask:

  Would you like to do this again sometime?

- Finally, ring the special bell and ask the child to raise his hand when he no longer hears it. Thank the child for spending this special time together.

Extensions into Daily Life

- Nature provides unique moments to have present-moment awareness. You can decide to experience being at the seashore in silence as you watch the waves or perhaps take some moments of silence and gaze at the clouds and then later reflect on what you saw. Having children find a favorite tree or a place they visit regularly is another way to honor the power of nature.

• So often in our harried days with our children it can be easy to not
  have time to really be present with one another. The next time your
  child is telling a story from his day, or absorbed in play, or simply
  sitting on your lap, give yourself the gift of a mindfulness break—
  stop and truly be present to whatever you can learn about who
  your child truly is.

📖 **Story Time**

Together read *The Listening Walk* by Paul Showers. In this book, a
young girl takes a listening walk with her father and her dog Major.
The setting is urban, and the environment is rich in sounds. Some
sounds are not so pleasant, such as the sound of cars, construction,
and other human noise activities. Other noises, such as the tapping of
Major's toenails on the sidewalk, a sprinkler, and the birds in the park,
are enriching. The book concludes by asking the readers to close the
book, close their eyes, and just listen: there are always sounds to hear.

You might introduce the book by saying:

*Let's read what happens when this little girl goes on a walk with her
father and her dog Major and discover all the sounds she hears. Let's
notice which ones we have heard before and which ones are new to us.*

Read the book out loud together and feel free to have your child
repeat the sounds that the little girl hears as you are reading.

After reading, discuss:

*What are some sounds the little girl heard that were sounds that people
made? What were some other sounds she heard? Which ones have you
ever heard? Which ones were new sounds for you?*

You might suggest that you take a minute and close your eyes and
notice all the different sounds you hear right now, as the book's clos-
ing suggests.

Another good book to read aloud is *The Seashore Book* by Charlotte
Zolotow. In this book, a boy asks his mother, "What is the seashore
like?" He lives in the mountains and has never seen the sea. His
mother lovingly describes what a day at the beach—full of color,
sounds, and sights—might be like. Both the words and the pictures

reinforce the gentle mood of the quiet story so that the boy and the book's readers can close their eyes and be there, too.

You might begin by saying:

I would like to read you a book about a boy who lives in the mountains and has never been to the beach. But his mother helps him imagine what it feels like to be at the seashore in his mind, and he begins to feel like he is really there. Let's read and notice what he sees and hears and feels on his imaginary journey.

After reading, discuss:

So what did the boy see at the beach? What did he hear? What else did he experience?

Have you ever imagined being some place in your mind without ever going to that certain place? Where would you like to imagine going right now? Let's close our eyes and imagine going there and see what happens.

If it is difficult for your child to imagine a place, you might suggest going in your minds to a peaceful place in nature that both of you have been to before. Ask what the child sees there, what he hears and feels if he reaches out his hands while sitting in one place or walking.

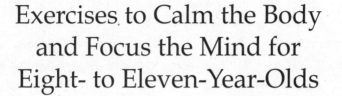

CHAPTER 4

Exercises to Calm the Body and Focus the Mind for Eight- to Eleven-Year-Olds

DEVELOPMENTAL ISSUES AFFECTING EIGHT- TO ELEVEN-YEAR-OLDS

Those of us who spend time with eight- to eleven-year-olds are often struck by their enthusiasm, energy, and imagination. While they still have that sense of wonder about the world around them from their earlier years, they also now have the rational skills to better understand that world—and themselves. For many parents this stage of childhood is therefore thought of as "the age of reason"—a time when children are beginning to be able to step back and reflect on their own thinking and actions. They are more aware of their thought processes and are more able to reflect on their behavior. As a result, their self-reporting about feelings and behavior becomes more reliable and accurate.

According to social psychologist Lev Vygotsky, social interaction is key for allowing the development of higher mental processes in eight- to eleven-year-olds. That is, they inhabit a world mediated by their sense of themselves in relationship to others—especially the significant adults in their world. The best learning experiences for this age therefore are those that involve a person they trust, someone who can provide assistance in learning a new skill. By teaching calming techniques such as those presented here, you'll not only take advantage of their emerging capacities but also help them to develop those very capacities.[1]

Along with these increased capacities and sense of themselves in relation to others, however, comes increased anxiety and worry. Children this age want to please and are therefore more sensitive to criticism, more fearful of new situations and tasks, and more likely to have performance anxiety. Learning calming strategies can give children of this age a very important tool for dealing with these difficult feelings.

WHAT TO REMEMBER ABOUT THIS AGE GROUP[2]

- Eight- to eleven-year-olds are energetic and imaginative. They need to have their energy focused on the task at hand, so be sure to set aside a time free of distraction and other demands for these activities.

- They learn best by having new knowledge and skills broken down one step at a time, so that they can meet with success at each level of complexity. Take it slowly and acknowledge that learning something new takes time and can be difficult.

- Since they sometimes want to give up and are very sensitive to criticism, you'll want to give them lots of positive feedback and encouragement each step of the way. Be sure to be specific when you offer praise.

- Children this age are very energetic and restless. While they need lots of physical release, they can also tire easily, so try to connect these activities to your child's natural rhythms when a quieting activity feels needed.

- Eight- to eleven-year-olds enjoy conversation with their parents. They are likely to talk easily when the setting is a familiar one and the conversation is open-ended. So be informal and conversational in tone. Likewise, they appreciate being asked questions that you as the adult genuinely do not know the answer to. Join in as equal partners on this exploratory journey with your child.

- Since children this age need the task at hand to make sense to them, it will be important for them to know why they are being asked to do these practices. Talk about the benefits of these contemplative practices whenever relevant.

EXERCISE

GETTING RELAXED: PROGRESSIVE MUSCLE RELAXATION

This exercise is Track 3 on the CD.

In this session children will be introduced to the idea of having a regular quiet time together with you to help calm their minds and relax their bodies. They will contrast how they feel in a relaxed state and in a stressful one, and they will better understand the "fight, flight, or freeze" response of their bodies. Then they will learn two techniques for releasing tension stored in their bodies: deep belly (also called diaphragmatic) breathing and progressive muscle relaxation. You'll help your child practice deep diaphragmatic breathing by using a balloon as a metaphor. She will also (optionally) be introduced to the biodot as a tool to gain awareness of her stress level. After a guided experience on the CD of a progressive muscle relaxation sequence, you'll introduce "reflection journals" — a place where both of you can regularly explore your feelings about the experience through art, writing, or other musings.

○○○ **BEFORE LISTENING TO THE CD**

What You'll Need

☐ Bell/chime (optional—see the Materials Checklist to order this item)

☐ Balloon

☐ A copy of the checklist "How Do I Feel When I Am Stressed?" and a pencil or pen

☐ The book *Building Emotional Intelligence*

☐ A CD player and the CD *Building Emotional Intelligence* cued up to "Getting Relaxed: Ages 8–11"

☐ Biodot card (optional—see the Materials Checklist to order this item)

☐ Two journals: one for you and one for your child (you can use paper, pens, crayons, and/or color markers and yarn or ribbon to make your own books, or buy notebooks with blank pages)

☐ A peaceful time and place to sit with your child, large enough to lie down comfortably

Time You'll Need: 30 Minutes

Concepts and Skills

Children will:

• contrast how they feel when they are calm versus when they are stressed

• practice using deep abdominal breathing to relax their bodies

• define stress as the body's response to something it feels as an emergency

• identify the situations that trigger the stress response within them

• experience relaxing their bodies through a progressive muscle relaxation exercise

What to Remember

• One of the best and most accessible ways to release tension and built-up stress is through deep belly or diaphragmatic breathing.

- In order to let go of tension through progressively tensing and releasing muscles, it is important to hold the tension in each area of the body for a few seconds and then let go of the contracted muscle quickly, rather than gradually.

Setting the Stage

- Begin by introducing your child to the new things you will be learning together through working with this book and CD. You might say something like:

  I'd like to take some special time with you, perhaps a couple of times a week, just to be still and have some quiet time together. During this time I wonder how you would feel about practicing some new ways of thinking and acting that we can both learn to help us handle stress — times when we are worried, angry, scared, or nervous. We'll learn some ways we can calm ourselves down and take control of our reactions. I've learned that when our minds are calm and our bodies are relaxed lots of good things can happen. We can pay attention better, make better decisions, and even feel healthier and happier.

- Mention to your child that you would like to always begin this special time together with a little silence. You will ring a chime once and ask her to listen to the sound of the chime until she hears it has stopped ringing and to raise her hand when she can no longer hear the chime — and you will do the same. Be patient with your child, especially if silence is something unusual for her. It may take time for her to adjust to the possibilities silence provides.

- Explain that you're going to spend some time noticing what your bodies feel like when you are worried or upset about something, and then notice how different your bodies feel when you are calm. You might start by saying:

  I would like both of us to think of a place that we have gone to several times, or maybe somewhere you have gone to only once, where you felt a deep sense of peace. It might be a place we've been to recently, or maybe it was a while ago. This is a place where you remember feeling completely calm, relaxed, and peaceful. Do you have a place that comes to mind? What is it?

After she has shared her place, then share yours.

- Now tell your child that you would like to take her on a journey in her imagination to that special peaceful place she just thought of. You might say the following:

    Let's see if we can go to that special place in our imagination. Would you be willing to try? Let's close our eyes and get comfortable. Imagine you are in this peaceful place right now. [Pause ten seconds.]

    Look around and notice what you see. Notice the colors and the shapes of things around you . . . Notice if you hear any sounds . . . any smells . . . If you stretch out your arm in your imagination, notice what your hand is touching and how it feels . . . Just take some time to really be present in this special place until I ring the chime. [Wait about fifteen seconds before ringing the chime.]

    Now let's slowly come back into the room and open our eyes. Were you able to imagine yourself in [name of the place]?

    How are you feeling right now? What are some things going on in your body?

    Elicit responses such as slow, comfortable breathing; relaxed muscles; a slower heartbeat; a sense of calm, etc. Acknowledge that these are some of the signs in our bodies when we are feeling relaxed.

- Next, ask your child to think about a time within the past few days when she felt very upset or stressed, frightened or nervous.

    Now I would like you to think about a time in the last several days when you felt very stressed. You were really upset. You might have been worried, angry, or frightened. It might have been a person that upset you, or a place — maybe you were at recess — or a situation — like taking a test — that upset or stressed you. Let's take a moment and see if you can think of something you would be willing to share with me. [Pause for a moment.] *Can you think of something? Where were you? Who were you with? What was happening?* [Discuss, and share a time you might have felt stressed, too.]

- Have a discussion about the physical symptoms of stress using the "How Do I Feel When I Am Stressed?" checklist on page 72.

  Now, thinking about that stressful time, let's give some thought to how our bodies feel when we are stressed. Let's take a look at this list I have here and check off everything that we remember feeling when we were in that stressed situation we thought of.

- Acknowledge that our minds and bodies react very differently when we are feeling stressed, and that sometimes we are able to notice those differences, but not always. Also, what bothers one person might be different from what bothers someone else.

Optional Biodot Activity

- You could introduce the biodots to help your child become more aware of her physiological response to different levels of stress. In our work with children, we have been quite successful using biodots to help children have a way in which they can receive immediate feedback about their level of stress. The biodot is a reasonably accurate, temperature-sensitive instrument. It changes color when subjected to variations in skin temperature. It works because blood flow to the extremities, such as the hands, is greatly reduced when we are in a stressed condition, and the biodot responds to such a change.

  Sometimes we know when we are feeling calm or upset, but sometimes we cannot tell clearly how we feel. Let me show you something called a biodot. [Put one on the web of your hand between the thumb and index finger.]

  This little dot changes colors depending on how stressed out or calm we feel inside. When we are experiencing stress, our hands feel cold because our tiny blood vessels called capillaries close down; when we are relaxed, our blood flow increases, and our hands get warmer. This little dot can read those kinds of changes in our bodies and change color accordingly.

  Ask your child to put a biodot on her hand.

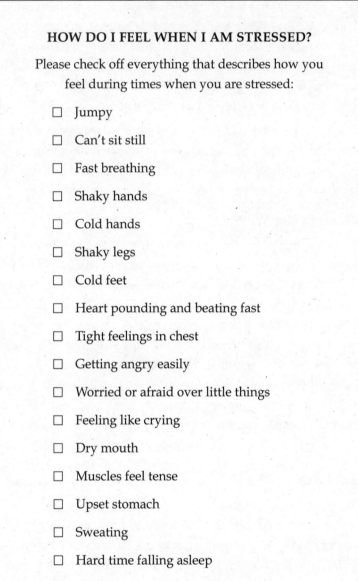

HOW DO I FEEL WHEN I AM STRESSED?

Please check off everything that describes how you
feel during times when you are stressed:

☐ Jumpy

☐ Can't sit still

☐ Fast breathing

☐ Shaky hands

☐ Cold hands

☐ Shaky legs

☐ Cold feet

☐ Heart pounding and beating fast

☐ Tight feelings in chest

☐ Getting angry easily

☐ Worried or afraid over little things

☐ Feeling like crying

☐ Dry mouth

☐ Muscles feel tense

☐ Upset stomach

☐ Sweating

☐ Hard time falling asleep

☐ Other _____

- Notice what colors your dots are and compare them to the chart on the biodot card. You may need to substitute some different words in order for your child to understand the meaning of each color:

  Purple: very calm

  Blue: tranquil (relaxed and peaceful)

  Green: calm (but not as calm as blue)

  Beige: involved (doing an activity like working or playing and feeling relaxed while doing it)

  Brown or black: stressed and very stressed (maybe very worried, anxious, or angry)

- Explain how the biodots can be useful in the next activity:

  We might want to keep our biodots on as we practice some ways to calm down, and we'll see if they change color. Would you like to do that? By the way, were you surprised what color your dot was when you put it on? Or not?

About the Fight/Flight/Freeze Response

- Explain why our bodies respond the way they do when we are stressed.

  Remember all those things we just checked off when we were talking about how our bodies and minds feel when we are upset? Those things happen to us whether we want them to or not, whenever we feel there is some kind of emergency. This is called the "fight, flight, or freeze" response. Why do you think it may be called that? [Pause for discussion.]

  Suppose, for example, it was long ago, when our ancestors lived very differently from the way we live today. They roamed the land searching for food in order to stay alive. Sometimes they would see a wild animal like a hungry mountain lion and had to fight or run for their lives! Try to imagine that. You see the lion, and your body becomes tense. You probably feel scared, so your heart starts beating faster to pump more oxygen to your muscles so that you can get ready for action. All these changes are happening because of one thought in your mind: danger! These changes help you either fight really hard against the lion or run away very, very fast. In that situation, the reaction that would happen in your body could actually save your life. You would be able to get ready to fight or run away. You also might freeze and not move at all, to keep yourself out of danger or perhaps because you were very frightened.

So this emergency reaction could help in a dangerous situation. But sometimes we think something is an emergency, but it is actually a false alarm, like the situation we thought about before where we felt stressed. Sometimes we can't tell the difference, and before we know it, we are getting ready for an emergency, but there isn't any danger. That is not good for our bodies, and that's why we are taking this time to practice how to calm our minds and relax our bodies. We can begin to learn how not to have so many false alarms.

Introduce Abdominal Breathing[3]

• Explain to your child that being aware of the way we breathe is a very important part of learning how to quiet the mind and relax the body when we feel upset.

One of the ways we can relax is by breathing really deeply. However, since breathing is something we do without thinking, we don't usually pay much attention to it, and we may not know if we're breathing deeply or not.

• Mention that you are going to take a few moments now to notice how we breathe. You might start by saying:

Let's get comfortable where we are sitting. You might want to gently close your eyes and relax. Now begin to notice your breath going in and out. In and out. [Pause while your child breathes in and out a few times.]

As you take in a breath, notice if you are taking it in through your nose . . . Your mouth? . . . Notice if your chest is getting bigger as you breathe in. Is any other part of your body rising? As you let out your breath, notice what part of your body is moving.

• Ask your child to open her eyes and together reflect on what she noticed.

- Mention to your child that one of the ways we know we're taking a deep breath is when we see our bellies going up and down, rather than just our chests. You might say:

    We might not always be taking in a deep breath when we breathe. I want to try something right now: an experiment. Stretch your arm out in front of you, higher than your shoulder, with your pointer (or index) finger up, as if you are pointing. Now move your finger back and forth like a windshield wiper. Do this about five times.

    Demonstrate with your finger and pause to give your child time to try it.

- Now ask the child about what happened to her breathing during this experiment. You might say:

    What did you notice about your breathing while you were doing this experiment? Were you breathing? Or holding your breath? Was your belly moving or just your chest?

- Since it's common to hold your breath while doing this experiment or to not breathe very deeply, this is an opportunity to point out that we often go through our day without breathing as deeply as we need to in order to relax our bodies and focus our minds.

    Lots of things in our day might interfere with how we breathe, making us not breathe deeply enough, whether or not we're aware of it. When we are distracted, or stressed, or even upset, we might not fully fill up our lungs and take in the oxygen we need for our bodies to stay healthy.

    [Inflate a balloon about one-quarter full.]

    Let me show you what I mean by using this balloon.

    When we don't breathe deeply — when only our chests move, and not our bellies — then we are filling our lungs only one-quarter of how full they can be, like this balloon is now. But when we breathe deeply, we fill up our lungs completely [fill up the balloon to capacity] and that makes our bellies rise and move in all directions, expanding like this balloon. When our lungs are full of air, we have all the oxygen we need for our bodies to do the work they need to do. It's important to let all the air out of our lungs as well. This breathing in and out deeply keeps us healthy, and it also relaxes us.

- Give deep breathing a try:

    Let's take in a breath right now and put both our hands on our bellies and see if our bellies can get bigger when we take in a breath. And when we let out the air, let's see if our bellies can go down. Ready? In 1, 2, 3, 4, 5, and out 1, 2, 3, 4, 5.

    When we take a really deep breath, not only do our chests go up, but our bellies do, too.

    This kind of breathing is called abdominal or diaphragmatic breathing. Our diaphragm is a muscle that divides our lungs from our lower organs, such as our stomach. When we belly breathe, we use our diaphragm to make more room for our lungs, so they can hold more air.

- Now try it again.

    Let's try it again. Breathe in to a count of 5: 1, 2, 3, 4, 5.

    Breathe out: 1, 2, 3, 4, 5

    Repeat a few more times until she has made her belly rise on the in-breath and go down on the out-breath. If the child is still not breathing deeply enough for her belly to rise, you can gently put your hand on her belly to help.

○○○ **LISTENING TO THE CD**

(Have the CD ready, cued "Getting Relaxed: Ages 8–11," for the next part of the activity.)

- Introduce the idea that you will be listening to a CD together that will guide you both through an experience of relaxing your bodies. Explain that the person's voice on the CD is a man named Daniel Goleman. You might say:

    So, one of the things we're going to be doing each time we have this special quiet time together is also to listen to a CD created by a man named Daniel Goleman, someone who is an expert on working with our emotions. He is going to help us learn different ways to quiet our minds and calm our bodies. On the CD he will help us pay attention to each part of our bodies, from our heads to our feet, and he will help us relax each of the parts of our bodies so that we can release the stress that may be there.

    He will ask us to tense up a certain group of muscles and then release that part of the body and let out the tension. The more we practice this, the easier it gets to become calmer or more relaxed when we are feeling stressed. Are you ready? I am going to do this with you, too.

    The CD is going to tell us to slowly notice different parts of our bodies. We're going to first tense up those parts real tightly and hold them for a while, and then we're going to quickly let those parts of our bodies go. Let's lie down and make ourselves comfortable before we begin.

    You might want to show the child what you mean, by clenching a fist and counting to five, then relaxing it and counting to ten.

- Start the CD.

Getting Relaxed: Progressive Muscle Relaxation (CD Script)

For eight- to eleven-year-olds: 9:33 minutes

We are going to spend a little time together learning how to release stress from your body by focusing on different parts of the body — one part at a time. We'll practice tensing different muscles and then notice how it feels to relax each part as well. This helps to release some of the tension that may be in your body, so you can feel even healthier and happier. So let's get ready to begin.

Lie down comfortably on the floor on your back. You may want to loosen any clothing that you feel is too tight, maybe take off your shoes, and just begin to relax with your arms at your sides and your legs straight out in front of you. Now gently close your eyes.

Begin to take some slow, deep breaths, and remember, as you breathe in, feel your belly and chest rising, and as you breathe out, say to yourself, "Relax," as your belly goes down.

Breathe in 1, 2, 3, 4, 5 . . . and out. Relax 1, 2, 3, 4, 5 . . . And again, in 1, 2, 3, 4, 5 . . . and relax, and you let the air out 1, 2, 3, 4, 5.

Try to listen to my voice as best you can and focus on what I am saying as you become more and more relaxed.

Imagine you have a soft piece of clay in your right hand. Now squeeze the clay in your right hand and make as tight a fist as you can, and make your whole right arm tense as well. Squeeze . . . squeeze . . . squeeze . . . Feel the tension in your right hand and arm.

Now quickly let your right hand go limp and let the imaginary clay drop to the floor. Let your right hand and arm completely let go and relax as I count to 10: 1, 2, 3, 4, 5, 6, 7, 8, 9, 10.

Feel your right hand and arm very warm and relaxed.

Now we are going to concentrate on your left hand and arm and do the same thing. So imagine you have a soft piece of clay in your left hand. Squeeze the piece of clay in your left hand and make as tight a fist as you can, as your whole left arm tenses as well. Squeeze . . . squeeze . . . squeeze . . . . Feel the tension in your left hand and arm.

Now quickly let your left hand go limp and let the imaginary clay drop to the floor. Let your left hand and arm completely let go and relax as I count to 10: 1, 2, 3, 4, 5, 6, 7, 8, 9, 10. Feel your left hand and arm very warm and relaxed. Good job. Your hands and arms are relaxed.

Now we are going to focus on relaxing your neck and your shoulders. Tense your shoulders by raising your shoulders up toward your ears and tighten your shoulders and neck and hold it as I count to 5: 1, 2, 3, 4, 5 . . . and relax. Let your shoulders drop away from your ears. Let your neck and shoulders relax as I count to 10: 1, 2, 3, 4, 5, 6, 7, 8, 9, 10. Just feel how relaxed your shoulders and neck are. Good job. Your shoulders and neck are relaxed.

Now turn your attention to your head and your face. See if you can tighten all the muscles in your face. Squeeze your eyes closed as tightly as you can and wrinkle your nose and your forehead and bite down hard and hold that tension as I count to 5: 1, 2, 3, 4, 5.

And let go and relax. Let your whole face and head be relaxed and soft. Still keep your eyes gently closed as your forehead, your nose, and your mouth are relaxed as I slowly count to 10: 1, 2, 3, 4, 5, 6, 7, 8, 9, 10 . . . Feel how relaxed your head and face are. Excellent. Your head and face are relaxed.

Next we will focus on our chest area. Take a deep breath in and fill your lungs up completely. Hold your breath for a moment . . . and let go . . . Let out the air and let your chest become relaxed as you continue to breathe in and out, deeply and slowly.

Next we will focus on your belly and the lower part of your body. Try to pull your belly in and bring it as much toward your back as you can as you make your whole lower part of your body tense. Make your belly as tight as you can and hold it until I count to 5: 1, 2, 3, 4, 5.

And relax and let go. Let your belly and all the muscles around it be soft and relaxed. Just continue to relax as I count to 10: 1, 2, 3, 4, 5, 6, 7, 8, 9, 10 . . . Feel how relaxed your stomach area is. Good job. The lower part of your body is relaxed.

Next we will focus on relaxing your legs and feet and even your toes.

Let's first start by tensing your right leg and foot and making it as stiff as you can — even curl up your toes on your right foot. Keep tensing your right leg and foot . . . and now let it go and relax your right leg and foot as I count to 10: 1, 2, 3, 4, 5, 6, 7, 8, 9, 10 . . . Feel how relaxed your right leg and foot feel.

Now let's do the same thing with your left leg and foot. Tighten your left leg and foot, making it as stiff as you can — even curl up your toes on your left foot. Keep tensing your left leg and foot . . . and now let go and relax your left leg and foot as I count to 10: 1, 2, 3, 4, 5, 6, 7, 8, 9, 10 . . .

Feel how relaxed both your legs and feet are. Feel the relaxation to the tips of your toes. Good job. Both your legs and feet are relaxed.

Now one last time: at the count of 3 try to tighten up your whole body all at once. Ready? 1, 2, 3 . . . Tighten and tense your whole body . . . Hold it . . . Squeeze . . . squeeze . . . squeeze . . . And let go. Let your whole body relax as you lie down and feel like you are melting into the floor. Feel the wave of warmth and relaxation throughout your whole body and let go of any last bit of tension.

Take a little time and notice if any part of your body might still feel tense or uncomfortable. Check in with each part of your body and ask yourself, Are my face and head relaxed? My chest area? My belly area? Both my arms to the tips of my fingers? Are my legs and feet relaxed? Just notice how relaxed your body is feeling right now.

Now gently begin to wiggle your toes and move your fingers and start to notice the sounds around you, and open your eyes and let your body take a nice big stretch and slowly begin to sit up and feel how relaxed you are.

Thanks for trying this out with me.

○○○ **AFTER LISTENING TO THE CD**

What to Do

- Help your child explore and reflect on what happened during the progressive muscle relaxation:

  How are you feeling right now? How are your arms feeling? Your legs? Let's notice our breath by putting our hands on our chests and bellies. How does that feel? What parts of your body were easy to relax? What parts were hard to relax? When might this exercise of relaxing different parts of our bodies be helpful in the next few days?

  It's helpful if you can together commit to another time you'll try this progressive muscle relaxation within the coming few days.

- Introduce the reflection journal as a tool for regular drawing and writing, as a way to reflect during these quiet times together. You might say:

  When we take this quiet time, I'd like to end it with drawing or writing in a journal about our experience together. I will do this, too. This is a way we can keep track of what happened when we tried these things out. We can decorate our journals any way we want. For today's journal entry, I thought perhaps we could draw or write about our special, peaceful place we thought of, or how our bodies looked or felt when they were relaxed.

  You might choose to draw to calming, soft music.

- When you both are finished, ask if your child would like to share her journal entry, and invite her to comment on anything she wants to. Share yours as well.

- Mention that you will spend this special time together a couple of times a week and maybe even more often later.

  Each time we take this special quiet time together, we'll do some activities and have a conversation. Then we'll listen to the CD and talk about what happened and draw or write in our journals. Once we have learned how to do the different calming activities that are on the CD, we'll probably just use the CD and our journals when we take our quiet time together.

Mention any commitments you've made for trying the progressive muscle relaxation again.

- End by explaining that you would like to close this special time together the same way that you started — by ringing a bell to signal the start of a moment of silence — and ask your child to close her eyes, raise her hand, and open her eyes when she no longer hears the bell.

- Ring the bell.

Extensions into Daily Life

- Refer to Guiding Principle 5: Integrate Rituals and New Routines (Chapter 2) for ways to continue to incorporate and reinforce the exercises learned. For example, your peace corner might now include the CD *Building Emotional Intelligence,* so your children can use it on their own whenever they need some quiet time.

- At this age, children begin to be more worried about all kinds of things and often have psychosomatic symptoms that accompany worry. Be on the lookout for symptoms of stress as listed in the "How Do I Feel When I Am Stressed" checklist (page 72), and help your child make a connection between those symptoms and people, places, and events in her life that are stress triggers. Then together commit to a time period to do the progressive muscle relaxation in a way that will best help her cope with stress.

- In addition to relaxing our bodies, progressive muscle relaxation can improve concentration. Since test-taking and other challenges can cause a lot of anxiety in this age group, try using the "Getting Relaxed: Progressive Muscle Relaxation" track on the CD in the morning before your child has a test or other challenge.

- Help your child use deep breathing as a way of quickly diffusing tension in the moment whenever she seems upset or overwhelmed, or as a regular practice before beginning homework, sports practice, or school. See the "Keep Calm" activity in Chapter 2.

- When you say good night to your child, try lying down next to her and attuning your breathing to hers. You can have an evening ritual of releasing some of the concerns of the day by naming each of them as you hold them one by one in a tightened fist and release the hand and let them float away. You might end with a few minutes of sharing some moments of the day that you are both thankful for.

- When taking a long car trip, or at other times when you and your child may be in a confined space for a while, you can talk through a shortened version of the progressive muscle relaxation experience by simply using a few words as cues. For example, you might say:

    Hands — squeeze . . . release . . . Feet and legs — squeeze . . . and release . . . Stomach in . . . and release . . . , etc.

📖 Story Time

Explain to your child that you would like to read a book out loud together entitled *A Quiet Place* by Douglas Wood. Although it looks like a book for younger children because it has pictures, the words and ideas are for children in this age group. Depending on your child's reading level, you may or may not decide to take turns reading the book out loud. The book begins with the words, "Sometimes a person needs a quiet place." The author takes the reader on a journey exploring different places that could be that quiet place. The book concludes with exploring what it is like to find that quiet place where you can think your own thoughts and feel your own feelings — "the one inside of you." You might begin by saying:

I have a book I'd like to read with you that talks about all the different places we could go to find a quiet place. The book has some beautiful pictures in it, but it might also have some difficult words to read. Shall we take turns reading it out loud together, and I will help you with the words you don't know?

As you begin reading the book, you might occasionally check in with your child about whether she has ever experienced a sense of stillness and quiet in the various places mentioned in nature or indoors.

After reading, discuss:

What is the message of this book? What is the author saying about the idea of finding a quiet place? How is the message of this story similar to what we did together when we listened to the CD?

Another good book to read aloud is *Cherish Today: A Celebration of Life's Moments* by Kristina Evans and Bryan Collier. The book's message explores how success is measured not necessarily by what you've achieved, but by how you handle the challenges along the way. It describes various stressors that could come a child's way. Pause throughout for reflection and discussion. You can ask open-ended questions, such as "When have *you* felt that way?" or "Does this remind you of anything you have experienced?"

EXERCISE

PAYING ATTENTION: MINDFULNESS

This exercise is Track 4 on the CD.

In this session, children will be introduced to the practice of mindfulness, which quiets the mind and focuses the attention using the breath as a focal point. Mindfulness is a way of paying attention to the present moment without judgment. You'll help your child bring his full attention and focus to some simple everyday activities, as well as a few fun and challenging ones. Then your child will experience feeling more mindful directly by bringing his full attention to the process of eating a raisin in slow motion, noticing how it feels in the present moment. The guided experience of mindfulness on the CD will introduce your child to the breath as an anchor for bringing his wandering mind back to attention. Then you'll explore ways to build mindfulness into your everyday life as you both record your experiences in your journal.

What You'll Need

☐ Bell/chime

☐ Two books with shiny, slippery covers about the same size

☐ A straight-backed chair for each person

☐ Two raisins for each person, with paper plates and napkins (if your child can't or won't eat raisins, use blueberries or grapes)

☐ Two reflection journals, and pens, crayons, or colored markers

☐ Biodot card

☐ The book *Building Emotional Intelligence*

☐ A CD player and the CD *Building Emotional Intelligence* cued up to "Paying Attention: Ages 8–11."

Time You'll Need: 30 Minutes

Concepts and Skills

Children will:

- articulate the meaning of "mindfulness" as being aware of what's happening as it's happening

- experience the concept of mindfulness using the different senses

- practice quieting the mind by using the breath as an anchor to bring attention to moment-to-moment awareness

- develop strategies for dealing with distractions during periods of stillness

What to Remember

- The thoughts, feelings, and sensations that come up during a mindfulness activity are not considered distractions. They are welcomed without judgment and become part of the experience.

- Children can learn to think of their breath as an anchor or home base. While their minds may drift like a boat, they can always return to the awareness of their breath as a way of bringing their attention to the present moment.

• During an experience of mindfulness, it is useful to label thoughts that come and go, using simple words like "hearing," "thinking," and "feeling." This process helps children to notice where their attention is, so they can then bring themselves back to their breath.

• Mindfulness can be practiced as a form of meditation and as a habit of awareness to cultivate during regular daily life. That is, we can approach any daily task — such as brushing our teeth, dressing, and eating — with the kind of full attention and wholeheartedness culti-vated in mindfulness.

Setting the Stage

• Remind your child that you would like to begin each session with a moment of silence. Explain that you will ring the bell once. Ask your child to close his eyes and then open his eyes and raise his hand when he doesn't hear the bell anymore. Ring the bell.

• You'll explore the concept of mindfulness through two challenge games that require us to be fully aware of our bodies. Explain that this next exercise will help your child quiet his mind, and that when we are calm, we are able to focus better and pay attention when we need to. You might introduce this session this way:

Remember when we had our last special quiet time together and we practiced relaxing our bodies? Today we are going to do something else that will help quiet our minds and focus our attention. We are going to practice something called "mindfulness." It sounds like a big word, but it's really a simple idea: mindfulness is knowing what you are feel-ing or thinking right now and paying attention to what you are doing as you are doing it . . . without judging or worrying about it. On any day of our lives, we do a lot of things without really noticing what we are doing — especially if we do it every day, like brushing our teeth or eating. When we are mindful, we bring our full selves and whole heart to any daily activity. Learning how to quiet our minds helps us to be able to focus our attention better, and that improves our concentration and ability to learn new things.

Play a Couple of Challenge Games

- Introduce the activity:

  I'd like to do a couple of fun activities right now with you. Let's explore what it feels like to be mindful and really focus and pay attention to what we are doing when we are doing it.

- In the first challenge activity, your child will try to pat his head while making a circular motion on his belly. Since this is a common coordination activity, he (and you) may have tried it before, but the goal here is not to do it correctly, but rather to simply experience being fully present in your body and in the moment while you try.

  Let's stand up and try a challenge activity: we're going to try to pat our heads with one hand while rubbing our bellies in the pattern of a circle with the other hand. [Demonstrate.] Have you ever tried this before? It sounds easy, but it can be a bit difficult to do. While we do it, let's just pay attention to how it feels to do it and not worry if we're doing it right or wrong. To start, take the hand that you don't write with. (Which one is that? It's your left hand if you're right-handed and your right if you're left-handed.) Now, with that hand, pat your head several times. While you're still patting your head, take your other hand and try to rub circles on your belly.

  Allow for laughter and several tries, since this can be very difficult to do.

- Once the child has done this successfully, you can progressively add more difficult challenges. You can also ask him to try this while standing on one foot. You could make it a little more challenging by asking him to count by twos while he is patting his head and rubbing his belly. Then try counting by threes starting at two while doing it (2, 5, 8, 11, etc.).

- Hint: Break the tasks into sections so that first he pats his head, then he adds rubbing his belly, then—once that is coordinated—he can try standing on one leg, and then perhaps add the counting part.

- Quickly process how that experience felt:

  How was that game for you? How hard or easy was it?

- Now try another challenge that will help your child to bring all of his attention to the task at hand and begin to realize that slowing down an activity may meet with greater success than doing it quickly. Take out the two books with the shiny, slippery covers.

    Now let's try another challenge game. This time, we're going to try to balance these two books on our heads while walking across the room. I'd like you to try to make it to the other side without the books falling off your head. Are you ready?

    Put both books, one on top of the other, on his head and begin. It may take a while for your child to realize that slower, more mindful walking usually meets with success more easily. You might ask:

    Can you think of anything you could do differently?

- When he has done this challenge successfully, you can debrief both exercises together.

    How did it feel to try to balance the books on your head while walking? What made it easier? How about the patting your head and rubbing your belly activity? How do these two experiences we have just had compare to how we usually go about our regular activities?

    Include your own insights in the discussion.

- Summarize and introduce the next activity:

    Being mindful means bringing all of your attention to something. These activities required us to bring all of our attention to the task we were doing — whether we were trying to coordinate patting and rubbing, or balancing the books. We were being mindful of how our bodies move and paying very close attention to what we were thinking and doing right in the moment.

Mindfully Eating a Raisin

- Explain that you are going to try out one more activity that requires really paying attention. This time your child will be eating a raisin in a very different way than either of you have experienced before. He will do it very slowly — as if he was eating it in slow motion — in order to explore what it's like to be mindful while we eat.

- Give your child and yourself two raisins each on a paper plate or napkin. You might want to give your child a chance to eat one raisin before continuing. You could say:

  I've got these raisins. I'm wondering if you'd like to taste one before we begin this activity.

- Now ask your child to bring all of his attention to the second raisin, first looking at it carefully, then touching it, but explain that he is not to put it in his mouth yet. After a few minutes of looking and touching silently, ask him for words that describe the raisin:

  What are some words to describe your raisin? What color is it? How big is it? Is it soft or hard? What does it smell like? What else do you notice about it?

- Have your child pick up the raisin and eventually put it into his mouth and eat it. You could say:

  Now, in slow motion, bring your hand with the raisin in it to your mouth and slowly put the raisin into your mouth and let it stay in your mouth without biting it yet; perhaps you can close your eyes and just feel it with your tongue as you move it around in your mouth. [Pause for ten seconds.] *Now slowly take one bite and start to really taste the raisin, noticing your tongue and teeth as you continue to chew it slowly. Notice what is happening to the raisin. What side of your mouth are you chewing on? Now slowly swallow it.*

- Ask:

  So what was that like? What did you notice? Any surprises? Was that hard or easy to do? Why?

  Share your own insights.

◯◯◯ **LISTENING TO THE CD**

(Have the CD ready, cued to "Paying Attention: Ages 8–11" for the next part of the activity.)

- Introduce the "Paying Attention: Mindfulness" exercise, an experience your child will be led through by Daniel Goleman.

  So far we've experienced different ways of being mindful. Now for the second time, we'll be listening to the CD where the man named Daniel Goleman will be leading us through another experience of training our minds to pay attention as our bodies also relax. This time we will be sitting still in our chairs and noticing what we are thinking and feeling each moment. He is going to tell us about using our breath to help us focus our attention.

  If you choose to use biodots, you can ask the following:

  Would you like to put your biodot on during this time? What color do you think it will be? Let's see.

  With or without a biodot, you can continue:

  Are we ready to turn the CD on?

- Have your child and yourself put on a biodot, if appropriate, then get comfortable in your chairs.

- Start the CD.

Paying Attention: Mindfulness (CD Script)

For eight- to eleven-year-olds: 7:50 minutes

In this activity of quieting the mind and relaxing the body, we are going to practice paying attention by bringing our full awareness to what's happening in the present moment. This is called mindfulness — being aware of all that's going on inside you and around you without judging it or worrying about it. In a moment, we are going to close our eyes and start by paying attention to our breath.

The breath can be like an anchor for you. You may know that an anchor is what holds a boat in place, keeping it safe, so it doesn't drift off in the ocean. Your thoughts and feelings can wander in different directions just like a boat does — but your breath can always be an anchor to bring your attention back to the present moment.

So let's begin by sitting comfortably in your chair with your feet flat on the ground, not crossed. Imagine there is an invisible string tied to a helium balloon attached to the top of your head . . . Your head and back are straight . . . and your arms and shoulders are relaxed . . . and your hands are resting gently on your lap.

Now, close your eyes and bring your attention to your breath, letting it flow in and out without effort . . . Don't try to control it. Just take normal breaths. Notice where your breath comes in. Is it your mouth? . . . Your nose? . . . And where it is leaving? . . . As you breathe in and out, notice your chest and belly getting bigger on the in breath and smaller on the out breath.

In . . . [pause 5 seconds] *and out* [pause 5 seconds] *. . . in . . .* [pause 5 seconds] *and out* [pause 5 seconds] *. . . in – taking in a deep breath, filling your chest and your belly . . . and out – letting out the air and feeling your belly and chest go down . . . And then just let your breathing be normal . . . Just take a little time to focus on your breathing and whenever you take a breath in, you may silently say to yourself, "In . . ." and when you take a breath out, silently say, "Out . . ."* [pause 15 seconds].

And now, if you notice that your mind has wandered, as can easily happen, gently notice what caught your attention . . . Is it a sound in the room? . . . Or maybe a feeling in your body? . . . When you notice you've wandered from your breath, just gently notice where your mind went . . . You can try naming what's happening . . . So, for example, if you notice a sound, you may silently say to yourself, "Sound . . ." without getting lost in what's making the sound.

So, let's tune in a bit to the sounds in the room right now – the sounds very near and the sounds farther away. Every time you hear a sound . . . whatever the sound is . . . just simply name what's going on by saying silently to yourself, "Sound . . ." Let's listen for a while right now . . . and every time you hear a sound, say to yourself, "Sound," and then come back to noticing your breath: in . . . out . . . in . . . out . . . [Long pause.]

Remember when you hear a sound, you don't even have to know for sure what the sound is. Just say to yourself, "Sound," and come back to your breath: in . . . out . . . in . . . out . . .

And now, as you are focusing on your breath, notice if your mind has any other thoughts or feelings. Tune in and ask yourself, "How am I feeling right now?" [Pause for 10 seconds.] *Am I noticing a certain part of my body?* [Pause for 20 seconds.] *Can I notice my thoughts coming and going?* [Pause for 20 seconds.]

Whenever you notice that your mind has wandered away from your breath, name to yourself what you're doing — like hearing sounds — and then bring your mind back to watching your breath: in . . . out . . . in . . . out . . .

So when you notice that your mind has a thought or a feeling, just name what's going on inside your mind. Say to yourself something like, "Daydreaming," or "Thinking" . . . and come back to your breath as the air goes in . . . and out . . . in . . . and out . . . [pause for 20 seconds].

Now begin to notice the chair you are sitting on, and notice your feet on the floor, and start to gently move your fingers and your toes . . . and slowly open your eyes, noticing how you are feeling right now.

Being mindful is something you can do not only when your eyes are closed — you can do lots of things mindfully. It simply means that you are really paying full attention to everything that is going on in the moment. You could even brush your teeth mindfully.

Thanks for trying this out with me.

○○○ **AFTER LISTENING TO THE CD**

What to Do

- Share how the experience of mindfulness was for you both. Possible debriefing questions:

  What sounds did you hear when we were asked to listen for sounds?

  How hard or easy was it to say to yourself, "Sound," when you heard a sound?

  What happened when you were asked to notice how you were feeling and to pay attention to your body? What part of your body did you notice?

  Was it easy or hard for you to keep bringing your mind back to your breath?

  Summarize any comments or insights and share what happened for you as well.

- Now pull out your reflection journals and remind your child how this special journal is one way that you both can remember what you've learned during your time together.

  Let's take a few minutes to draw or write about today's experience. I was thinking that we might draw or write about one of our favorite parts of today's quiet time and also what was easy and what was difficult about today's time together.

- Discuss a few ways that your child might be able to be mindful — or really pay close attention to something he does all the time — a daily routine, perhaps. You might ask your child to think of something he is going to do before he goes to sleep tonight that he could do mindfully, e.g., brush his teeth. Ask:

  Would you like to do this again sometime? Can you think of something we can commit together to do mindfully before we go to bed tonight?

- Finally, ring the special bell and ask your child to close his eyes and then open his eyes and raise his hand when he no longer hears it. Thank the child for spending this special time together.

Extensions into Daily Life

- Coloring can be a soothing and calming activity for children this age. You can try the *Kids Mandala Coloring Set* by Monique Mandali. Mandalas are geometric or symbolic patterns, usually in the form of a circle. Coloring these circles fosters the focused attention of mindfulness.

- Go on a mindfulness walk in nature with your child. Plan a designated time period to walk in silence, simply noticing the smells, sounds, and sights you pass. For a first time taking this sort of walk in nature, it's helpful to focus your child's attention on the present moment by deciding together on one thing you may particularly look for. Depending on the season, it might be spiderwebs or ladybugs. Suggest that you walk in silence, but either of you can point if you spot the special thing you are looking for.

- Another nature experience that can happen even on a vacant lot is a "micro-hike." Give your child a magnifying glass and a piece of string about four yards long. You can each do this activity separately. Span the string on any place on the ground, and start to notice what you can see as you keep your eyes no higher than a foot from the ground, slowly crawling along the length of the string. At the end of the string, share what each of you has discovered. You may even want to go on each other's micro-hike.[4]

- Think about transitions as a special opportunity to slow down the pace and take a mindfulness break. For example, before school, incorporate a daily ritual of a moment of silence and then perhaps share a hope you both have for the day ahead. If your child walks to school, she can use part of her walk as an opportunity to walk in silence and focus completely on every step and sensation.

- So often in our harried days with our children it can be easy to not have time to really be present with one another. The next time your child is telling you about his day, or absorbed in a task, or simply sitting near you, give yourself the gift of a mindfulness break—stop and truly be present to whatever you can learn about who your child truly is.

📖 Story Time

Together read *Everybody Needs a Rock* by Byrd Baylor and Peter Parnall. In this book, the author lays out the reasons why "everybody needs a rock" and the rules for finding your very own perfect rock. Essentially, this book pays homage to the gifts of nature that are ours to experience if we simply slow down and pay attention.

You might introduce the book by saying:

I have a book I would like to read with you. It is called Everybody Needs a Rock. *In this book, the author, Byrd Baylor, talks about why we all need a rock. She brings our attention to what is special about each and every rock you look at. And still, she points out, you need to weigh all the options before choosing the right rock for you. Can you think of a time you decided to pick up and keep a rock because it felt special to you? Where were you?*

Read the book out loud together.

After reading, discuss:

What were some of the author's rules about finding a special rock? What would some of your rules be for finding the perfect rock?

Shortly after reading the book, you might want to go for a walk to find your own special rock. Walk in silence so that you each have your own opportunity to bring focused attention to selecting just the right rock for you. Afterward ask:

Tell me about the rock you chose. Why is it special to you, and what does it remind you of?

Another good book to read aloud is *Peaceful Piggy Meditation* by Kerry Lee MacLean. The book describes the various benefits that taking a regular quiet time can bring, and points these out in a convincingly creative way. Once your child begins to practice these calming strategies more regularly, this would be a good time to read the book together and reflect together, asking yourselves the question: "Have there been times since we've been taking this quiet time that these new skills helped us in the situations Miss Piggy found herself in?"

CHAPTER 5

Exercises to Calm the Body and Focus the Mind for Twelve-Year-Olds and Up

DEVELOPMENTAL ISSUES AFFECTING TWELVE-YEAR-OLDS AND UP

If there is one word that characterizes adolescence, it would be "change." Adolescents are changing quickly—emotionally, physically, intellectually, socially, and spiritually. Central to this metamorphosis is the young person's sense of his emerging self as an adult, not a child. While this transformation is a normal part of growing up that we all must navigate, nothing quite equals adolescence in terms of the stress and demands placed on the young person and his parents; nor does any stage quite offer the same opportunity, anticipation, and sense of possibility that adolescence does.

Adolescents have many sources of stress in their lives. At the same time that their bodies are changing in bewildering ways, they are feeling self-conscious about the judgment of others—especially of their peers, who may not always be so kind. Furthermore, they are measuring themselves against yardsticks provided by a culture with often unrealistic ideals about appearance and achievement. Added to this is the confusing pressure of conformity, which often involves risky behaviors that may be associated with adulthood, but for which they may not yet fully understand the consequences.

Adolescents are on a roller coaster with their emotions, and calming techniques can be very helpful. They need both the ability to concentrate more and the ability to balance their emotions. Young people this age also have a strong need for physical release, just at the time that our schools and culture demand longer periods of sitting for instruction and place growing demands on their time.

Adolescents no longer inhabit a world defined by grown-ups, but rather one defined by their peers. While they push us away, they in fact still need the guidance and understanding of the significant adults in their lives to help them navigate this tumultuous time. Young people also need time for self-reflection and to turn inward in order to define their own sense of meaning and purpose for their lives, yearnings that are inherent in this developmental stage. By sharing these calming strategies, as well as being a companion and guide throughout the process, you'll give your children the important skills and opportunities they need to defuse the many stressors they may encounter.

WHAT TO REMEMBER ABOUT THIS AGE GROUP

- Adolescents have a strong need for the sort of self-determination they associate with adulthood. They'll need their own clear reasons and motivations to do this work, rather than any externally motivated reason such as that provided by a parent. Provide opportunities to discuss the benefits of these practices, ranging from improving social skills to gaining more self-confidence. Model the skills yourself, build rituals into your home, and let your child make the decision to try the skills on the CD. Suggest the idea of trying these techniques and then let go of your own agenda about how it will work out.

- Since young people this age can have fragile self-esteem, give your child plenty of time, opportunity, and support to learn and master the skills. One of the key ways children this age can enhance their self-esteem is by mastering new skills. Concentrate on finding an approach that sets your child up for success, or she may reject the whole idea as something not worth doing.

- Young people this age have a strong need to belong. If your child is interested, you might suggest he find a buddy who is willing to try out some of these techniques with him and you.

- Young people possess sensitive radar and are on the lookout for hypocrisy in adults. They'll respond positively if you model integrating these techniques into your lifestyle. Yet they also have a great need to make their own choices about whether they try them.

- Since adolescents are so self-conscious about the physical changes in their bodies (which to varying degrees can greatly affect their self-esteem), try not to point out anything about how your child holds her body or posture or how stress is affecting her physical appearance, even if you are merely trying to be helpful. However, if an opportunity presents itself, feel free to bring up your own experience with the CD. Sharing of this kind may spark some interest.

- Support your child in finding opportunities for self-reflection by giving him the time, privacy, and autonomy he may need to do this work. The list in the box "Ideas That Can Help Reduce Stress" (page 120) may be useful in expanding his repertoire.

- Adolescents thrive on rituals that acknowledge their growing independence and passage into adulthood. Consider simple ways you might acknowledge your child's mastery of these skills. Perhaps a symbol from nature or a special outing together might be the perfect way to acknowledge the internalization of these skills and your child's growing mastery and ability to care for herself.

    Since young people this age are such great leaders and problem solvers, they can serve as mentors or guides to younger children in the process of learning these skills, especially if you have children of different ages in your family.

☼ EXERCISE

GETTING RELAXED:
PROGRESSIVE MUSCLE RELAXATION AND BODY SCAN

This exercise is Track 5 on the CD.

In this session young people will be introduced to the idea of having a regular quiet time together to help calm their minds and relax their bodies. They will contrast how they feel in a relaxed state and in a stressful one, and they will better understand the "fight, flight, or freeze" response of their bodies. Then they will learn three techniques for releasing tension stored in their bodies: deep belly or diaphragmatic breathing, progressive muscle relaxation, and a body scan. You'll help your child practice deep diaphragmatic breathing by using a balloon as a metaphor. She will also (optionally) be introduced to the biodot as a tool to gain awareness of her stress level. After a guided experience on the CD of a progressive muscle relaxation and body scan sequence, you'll introduce "reflection journals"—a place where both of you can regularly explore your feelings about the experience through art, writings, or other musings.

○○○ **BEFORE LISTENING TO THE CD**

What You'll Need

☐ Bell/chime (optional — see the Materials Checklist to order this item)

☐ Balloon

☐ A copy of the checklist "How Do I Feel When I Am Stressed?" and a pencil or pen

☐ The book *Building Emotional Intelligence*

☐ A CD player and the CD *Building Emotional Intelligence* cued up to "Getting Relaxed: Ages 12 and Up."

☐ Biodot card (optional — see the Materials Checklist to order this item)

☐ Two journals: one for you and one for your child (you can use paper, pens, crayons, and/or color markers and yarn or ribbon to make your own books, or buy notebooks with blank pages)

☐ A peaceful time and place to sit with your child, large enough to lie down comfortably

Time You'll Need: 35 Minutes

Concepts and Skills

Young people will:

• contrast how they feel when they are calm versus when they are stressed

• practice using deep abdominal breathing to relax their bodies

• define stress as the body's response to something it perceives as an emergency

• identify situations that trigger the stress response within them

• experience relaxing their bodies through a progressive muscle relaxation and body scan

What to Remember

• One of the best and most accessible ways to release tension and built-up stress is through deep belly or diaphragmatic breathing.

- In order to let go of tension through progressively tensing and releasing muscles, it is important to hold the tension in each area of the body for a few seconds and then let go of the contracted muscle quickly, rather than gradually.

Setting the Stage

- Begin by introducing your child to the new things you will be learning together through working with this book and CD. You might say something like:

I've been listening to a CD these past couple of weeks that has been helping me learn some new ways I can calm myself down and handle my stress better. I am wondering if you would be willing to try this out with me. [You might also ask if she would like to invite a friend to join her.] *I find it so important to be able to learn how to calm my mind and relax my body when I need to. I would have loved to learn to be more in control of my mind and my body when I was growing up. Scientists have been finding out that knowing how to deal with stress is important for our health, and the sooner we learn ways to deal with stress the better. They say that being able to manage our stress has all kinds of benefits. It can improve our attention, so we can concentrate better. That can help us more easily remember all the things we know — when we take a test, for example. We can even make better decisions, be more creative, and, of course, be healthier and happier. Did you know that I learned that the main reason people go to doctors in the United States has to do with things that relate to dealing with their stress?*[1]

So, would you be willing to try this out with me? What I would like to do first in order to get ready to listen to the CD is to have a conversation about some of the things that the CD is going to introduce, then both of us will listen to the CD and try out the calming exercise, and then we can take a little time afterwards to reflect on what we experienced. I am hoping we can take this private quiet time together a couple of times a week. After we've tried it once, we'll see how you feel about whether you would like to continue.

- Mention to your child that you would like to begin this special time together with a little silence. You will ring a chime once and ask her to listen to the sound of the chime until she hears it has stopped ringing and to raise her hand when she can no longer hear the chime, and you will do the same. Silence may be something unusual for her — and it could take time for her to adjust to the possibilities silence provides.

- Ask your child to think about a time within the past few days when she felt very upset or stressed:

  I would like us both to think about a time in the last several days when each of us felt very stressed and were really upset. You might have been worried, angry, or frightened. It might have been a person that upset you, or a place (maybe you were on the bus going to school), or a situation (like taking a test) that upset or stressed you. Let's take a moment and see if we both can think of something to share. [Pause for a moment.]

  Can you think of something? Where were you? Who were you with? What was happening?

  Discuss and share a time you might have felt stressed, too.

  Have a discussion about the definition of stress and the physical symptoms of stress using the "How Do I Feel When I Am Stressed?" checklist.

  Now, thinking about that stressful time, let's give some thought to how our bodies feel when we are stressed. What are some signs of stress?

- Brainstorm some of these signs together before showing the "How Do I Feel When I Am Stressed?" checklist. Then combine your brainstormed list with some of the things on the checklist. Notice which things you have already mentioned and which things you did not think of.

- Acknowledge that our minds and bodies react very differently when we are feeling stressed, and that sometimes we are able to notice those differences, but not always. Also, what bothers one person might be different from what bothers someone else.

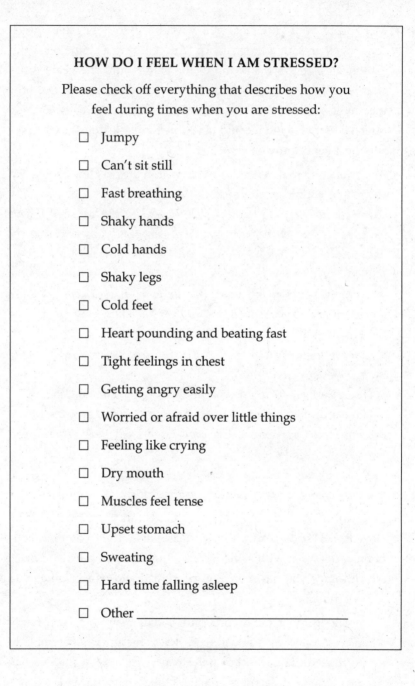

HOW DO I FEEL WHEN I AM STRESSED?

Please check off everything that describes how you
feel during times when you are stressed:

☐ Jumpy

☐ Can't sit still

☐ Fast breathing

☐ Shaky hands

☐ Cold hands

☐ Shaky legs

☐ Cold feet

☐ Heart pounding and beating fast

☐ Tight feelings in chest

☐ Getting angry easily

☐ Worried or afraid over little things

☐ Feeling like crying

☐ Dry mouth

☐ Muscles feel tense

☐ Upset stomach

☐ Sweating

☐ Hard time falling asleep

☐ Other _____

•Begin to develop the understanding that stress is not stress until we experience it in our bodies and have a physiological reaction in our bodies. Explain:

Stress is a result of what happens in our bodies. The things that cause stress — people, places, or events — are not actually stress until the mind sees it that way and the body responds. Stress is the body's response to certain demands. These demands are called stressors.

A situation that can cause us to feel stressed is first something outside of our bodies — it can be a person, place, or event. If we respond to this person, place, or event by feeling upset and tense, then we call that a "stress trigger." The situation triggered an automatic response in our bodies that is called the "fight, flight, or freeze" response. We'll talk about that in a few minutes. So, for example, what are a few of your top stress triggers — things that get you upset quite quickly?

You may wish to share some of your stress triggers as well.

Optional Biodot Activity

• You might introduce the biodot to help your child become more aware of her physiological response to different levels of stress. In our work with children, we have been quite successful using biodots in order to give them immediate feedback about their level of stress. The biodot is a reasonably accurate, temperature-sensitive instrument. It changes color when subjected to variations in skin temperature. It works because blood flow to the extremities, such as the hands, is greatly reduced when we are in a stressed condition, and the biodot responds to such a change.

Sometimes, we know when we are feeling calm or upset, but sometimes we cannot tell clearly how we feel. Let me show you something called a biodot. [Put one on the web of your hand between the thumb and index finger.]

This little dot changes colors depending on how stressed out or calm we feel inside. When we are experiencing stress, our hands feel cold because our tiny blood vessels called capillaries close down; when we are relaxed, our blood flow increases, and our hands get warmer. This little dot can read those kinds of changes in our bodies and change color accordingly. Sometimes we may already be aware of what our body is feeling.

Ask your child to put a biodot on his hand.

• Notice what colors your dots are and compare them to the chart on the biodot card:

Purple: very calm

Blue: tranquil (relaxed and peaceful)

Green: calm (but not as calm as blue)

Beige: involved (doing an activity like working or playing and feeling relaxed while doing it)

Brown or black: stressed and very stressed (maybe very worried, anxious, or angry)

• Explain how the biodots can be useful in the next activity:

We might want to keep our biodots on as we practice some ways to calm down, and we'll see if they change color. Would you like to do that? By the way, were you surprised what color your dot was when you put it on? Or not?

About the Fight/Flight/Freeze Response

• Explain why our bodies respond the way they do when we are stressed:

Remember all those things we just talked about, how our bodies and minds feel when we are stressed? Those things happen to us whether we want them to or not, whenever we feel there is some kind of emergency, whether it is really an emergency or not. This is called the "fight, flight, or freeze" response. This stress response happens automatically when we feel we are in danger. What do I mean when I say something happens automatically? [Pause for discussion.]

Yes, it means that we don't have to try to make it happen; it happens by itself. In fact, we are born with the "fight, flight, or freeze" response in us.

Suppose, for example, you are roaming in a forest one day and all of a sudden you hear sounds, and before you know it, you see a black bear staring at you! Try to really picture that. What do you imagine would start going on in your mind and your body? [Pause for discussion.]

Your heart would start beating faster to pump more oxygen to your muscles so that you could get ready for action. You might feel dizzy and sweaty. All these changes are happening because of one thought in your mind: danger! These changes help you either fight really hard against the bear or run away very, very fast. In that situation, the reaction that would happen in your body could actually save your life. You would be able to get ready to fight or run away. You also might freeze, or not move at all, to keep yourself out of danger or perhaps because you were very frightened. And then, all of a sudden, imagine the bear turns around and walks away, and you can breathe a sigh of relief!

So this emergency reaction really could help in a genuinely dangerous situation. For example, if you are about to cross the street on a green light, but a car doesn't stop, and you have to jump to get out of the way so you don't get hit — then it's a good thing to have the "fight, flight, or freeze" response. It can save your life.

But sometimes we think something is an emergency, and it is really a false alarm, like the situation we thought about before when we felt stressed. Sometimes we can't tell the difference, and before we know it, we are getting ready for an emergency — even though there isn't any real danger. When the stress response goes off, our brains release all kinds of chemicals so that we have the strength to face a dangerous situation. But when it's not really a dangerous situation, these chemicals start to make our bodies weaker, not stronger, and they start to affect our health.

That's why we are taking this time to practice how to calm our minds and relax our bodies. We can cut down on the number of false alarms. We can learn to change how we react to stress, and thereby gain a little more control over our emotions.

Introduce Abdominal Breathing[2]

• Explain to your child that being aware of the way we breathe is a very important part of learning how to quiet the mind and relax the body when we are stressed. However, since breathing is something we do automatically, we don't pay much attention to it. Yet our breath brings us all kinds of things that we need — energy, clear thinking, and better health. Also, when we learn to work with our breathing, we may be able to actually change our mood or release stress from our bodies. Mention to your child that you are going to have her take a few moments now to notice more carefully how she breathes. Ask her to do the following to begin to tune in to her breath and learn some new things about it.

One of the ways we can relax is by breathing really deeply. However, since breathing is something we do automatically also, we don't usually pay much attention to it and may not know if we're breathing deeply or not.

We might not always be taking in a deep breath when we breathe. I want to try something right now: an experiment. Stretch your arm out in front of you, higher than your shoulder with your pointer (or index) finger up, as if you are pointing. Now move your finger back and forth like a windshield wiper. Do this about five times.

Demonstrate with your finger and pause to give your child time to try this.

• Now ask your child what happened to her breathing during this experiment. You might say:

What did you notice about your breathing while you were doing this experiment? Were you breathing? Or holding your breath? Was your belly moving or just your chest?

• Since it's common to hold your breath while doing this experiment or to not breathe very deeply, this is an opportunity to point out that we often go through our day without breathing as deeply as we need to relax our bodies and focus our minds.

Lots of things in our day might interfere with how we breathe, making us not breathe deeply enough, whether or not we're aware of it. When we are distracted, or stressed, or even upset, we might not fully fill up our lungs and take in the oxygen we need for our bodies to stay healthy.

[Inflate a balloon about one-quarter full.]

Let me show you what I mean, by using this balloon.

When we don't breathe deeply — when only our chests fill up, but our bellies don't rise — then we are filling our lungs to only one-quarter of how full they can be, like this balloon is now. But when we breathe deeply, we fill up our lungs completely [fill up the balloon to capacity] and that makes our bellies rise, and move in all directions, expanding like this balloon. When our lungs are full of air, we have all the oxygen we need for our bodies to do the work they need to do. It's important to let all the air out of our lungs as well.

- Explain to your child that the more oxygen we breathe in each time we inhale, the better it is for our bodies in terms of staying healthy and giving us the energy we need. The same is true for our exhalations. When we exhale, or let the breath out, we release something called carbon dioxide. And the more carbon dioxide we can let out on each breath, the healthier we stay. Then we begin the cycle again — bringing fresh air into our lungs on the inhalation and releasing stale air as carbon dioxide through exhalation. It is good for our bodies to breathe deeply, taking in as much air and letting out as much air as we can. It is like giving our bodies the food we need to stay alive.

  Sometimes, however, if we are holding too much stress in our bodies, we forget to breathe in this way, especially when we get older.

- Give deep breathing a try:

  Let's take in a breath through our noses right now with our mouths closed and put both our hands on our bellies and see if our bellies rise when we take in a breath. And when we let out the air, let's see if our bellies fall. Ready? In 1, 2, 3, 4, 5, and out 1, 2, 3, 4, 5.

  When we take a really deep breath, not only do our chests expand, but our bellies do, too.

  This kind of breathing is called abdominal or diaphragmatic breathing. Do you know where the diaphragm is in the body? [Pause for discussion.] The diaphragm is a muscle that divides our lungs from our lower organs, such as our stomach. It is a thin sheet of muscle fiber and it expands from the front to the back and side to side. It is shaped like a dome. When we inhale, the diaphragm flattens and tightens.

When we exhale, the diaphragm returns to its relaxed position, which is right between the lungs. When we belly breathe, we use our diaphragm to make more room for our lungs, so they can hold more air.

• Now try it again.

   Let's try it again. Breathe in to a count of 5: 1, 2, 3, 4, 5. Breathe out: 1, 2, 3, 4, 5.

   Repeat a few more times until she has made her belly rise on the in-breath and fall on the out-breath. If your child is still not breathing deeply enough for her belly to rise, you can gently put your hand on her belly to help.

⊙⊙⊙ **LISTENING TO THE CD**

(Have the CD ready, cued to "Getting Relaxed: Ages 12 and Up," for the next part of the activity.)

- Introduce the idea that you will be listening to a CD together that will guide you both through an experience of relaxing your bodies. Explain that the person's voice on the CD is a man named Daniel Goleman. You might say:

    So, one of the things we're going to be doing each time we have this special quiet time together is also to listen to a CD by a man named Daniel Goleman. He has written a lot of best-selling books on how to work with our emotions. He is going to teach us a technique that will help us to quiet our minds and calm our bodies. For the technique on the CD we are about to experience today, he is going to help us focus on each part of our bodies, from our heads to our feet, and he will help us relax each of these parts of our bodies so that we can release the stress that may be there.

    He will ask us to tense up a certain group of muscles and then release that part of the body and let out the tension. The more we practice this, the easier it gets to become calmer or more relaxed when we are feeling stressed. We sometimes can't control the things or people around us that make us stressed out, but we can control our response to them. That is what we are learning how to do. Are you ready? I am going to do this with you, too.

    The CD is going to tell us to slowly notice different parts of our bodies. We're going to first tense those parts up real tightly and hold them for a while, and then we're going to quickly let those parts of our bodies go. Then at the end of this section, Mr. Goleman is going to ask us to tune into our bodies one more time by bringing our attention to different parts without tensing our muscles. He will ask us to use just our minds and let go of any other tension we may feel in our bodies. Let's lie down and make ourselves comfortable before we begin.

    You might want to show your child what you mean, by clenching a fist and counting to five, then relaxing it and counting to ten.

- Start the CD.

Getting Relaxed: Progressive Muscle Relaxation (CD Script)

For ages twelve and up: 12:32 minutes

Today we are going to learn a way to relax our bodies and quiet our minds. The calming activity we will practice today involves tensing and relaxing the different muscle groups in our bodies. We are also going to begin to notice a little more deeply what parts of our bodies feel more relaxed and where we hold most tension in our bodies. This exercise will help us to learn how to relax different parts of our bodies, so we can ease tense muscles whenever we feel we need to. It's called progressive muscle relaxation, or body scanning. By progressive, we mean that we are going to progress or move through the whole body, paying attention to different parts of the body, moving from one part to the next, tensing and relaxing each different muscle group.

After going through the tensing and relaxing exercises, we'll go through our bodies one more time, becoming aware of how each part of the body feels, what parts of the body feel more relaxed and what parts of the body still need to relax. That's the part where we'll scan our bodies. That's why it's also called a body scan.

So let's get ready to begin.

Lie down comfortably on the floor on your back. You may want to loosen any clothing that you feel is too tight, maybe take off your shoes, and just begin to relax with your arms at your sides and your legs straight out in front of you. Now gently close your eyes.

Begin to take some slow, deep breaths, and as you breathe in, feel your belly and chest rising, and as you breathe out, say to yourself, "Relax," as your belly goes down.

Breathe in 1, 2, 3, 4, 5 . . . and out 1, 2, 3, 4, 5 . . . and again in 1, 2, 3, 4, 5 . . . and relax as you let the air out 1, 2, 3, 4, 5.

Try to listen to my voice as best you can and focus on what I am saying as you become more and more relaxed. If at first you have trouble staying still, that's perfectly natural. It should get easier and easier to be more still.

Let's now imagine you have a soft piece of clay in your right hand. Now squeeze the clay in your right hand and make as tight a fist as you can, and make your whole right arm tense as well. Squeeze . . . squeeze . . . squeeze . . . Feel the tension in your right hand and arm.

Now quickly let your right hand go limp and let the imaginary clay drop to the floor. Let your right hand and arm completely let go and relax as I count to 10: 1, 2, 3, 4, 5, 6, 7, 8, 9, 10. Feel your right hand and arm very warm and relaxed.

Now we are going to concentrate on your left hand and arm and do the same thing. So imagine you have a soft piece of clay in your left hand. Squeeze the piece of clay in your left hand and make as tight a fist as you can as your whole left arm tenses as well. Squeeze . . . squeeze . . . squeeze . . . Feel the tension in your left hand and arm.

Now quickly let your left hand go limp and let the imaginary clay drop to the floor. Let your left hand and arm completely let go and relax as I count to 10: 1, 2, 3, 4, 5, 6, 7, 8, 9, 10. Feel your left hand and arm very warm and relaxed. Good job. Your hands and arms are relaxed.

Now we are going to focus on relaxing your neck and your shoulders. Tense your shoulders by raising your shoulders up toward your ears and tighten your shoulders and neck and hold it as I count to 5: 1, 2, 3, 4, 5 . . . and relax. Let your shoulders drop away from your ears. Let your neck and shoulders relax as I count to 10: 1, 2, 3, 4, 5, 6, 7, 8, 9, 10. Just feel how relaxed your shoulders and neck are. Well done. Your shoulders and neck are relaxed.

Now turn your attention to your head and your face. See if you can tighten all the muscles in your face. Squeeze your eyes closed as tightly as you can and wrinkle your nose and your forehead and bite down hard and hold that tension as I count to 5: 1, 2, 3, 4, 5 . . . and let go and relax. Let your whole face and head be relaxed and soft. Still keep your eyes gently closed as your forehead, your nose, and your mouth are relaxed as I slowly count to 10: 1, 2, 3, 4, 5, 6, 7, 8, 9, 10 . . . Feel how relaxed your head and face are. Nice job. Your head and face are relaxed.

Next we will focus on our chest area. Take a deep breath in and fill your lungs up completely. Hold your breath for a moment . . . and let go . . . Let out the air and let your chest become relaxed as you continue to breathe in and out, deeply and slowly.

Next we will focus on your belly and the lower part of your body. Try to pull your belly in and bring it as much as you can toward your back as you make the whole lower part of your body tense. Make your belly as tight as you can and hold it until I count to 5: 1, 2, 3, 4, 5 . . . and relax and let go. Let your belly and all the muscles around it be soft and relaxed. Just continue to relax as I count to 10: 1, 2, 3, 4, 5, 6, 7, 8, 9, 10. Feel how relaxed your stomach area is. Good job. Your lower part of your body is relaxed.

Next we will focus on relaxing your legs and feet and even your toes.

Let's first start by tensing your right leg and foot and making it as stiff as you can — even curl up your toes on your right foot. Keep tensing your right leg and foot . . . and now let it go and relax your right leg and foot as I count to 10: 1, 2, 3, 4, 5, 6, 7, 8, 9, 10. Feel how relaxed your right leg and foot have become.

Now let's do the same thing with your left leg and foot. Tighten your left leg and foot, making it as stiff as you can — even curl up your toes on your left foot. Keep tensing your left leg and foot . . . and now let go and relax your left leg and foot as I count to 10: 1, 2, 3, 4, 5, 6, 7, 8, 9, 10. Feel how relaxed both your legs and feet feel. Feel the relaxation to the tips of your toes. Good job. Both your legs and feet are relaxed.

Now one last time — at the count of 3 try to tighten up your whole body all at once. Ready? 1, 2, 3 . . . Tighten and tense your whole body . . . hold it . . . squeeze . . . squeeze . . . squeeze. And let go. Let your whole body relax as you lie down and feel you're melting into the floor. Feel the wave of warmth and relaxation throughout your whole body and let go of any last bit of tension.

Now we're going to use the body scan to go through our bodies one more time and become aware of how relaxed or tense we may still feel. Make yourself as comfortable as you can. I am going to ask you to take a moment to notice any part of your body that might still be holding any tension. As you begin to scan your body, notice first how you are breathing. Making sure your breathing is deep belly breathing, the kind you practiced at the beginning of this session.

Now start with your feet. Notice what's happening with your feet. Is there any tension in your feet? If you find any places of tension, silently and gently ask your feet to relax and let go.

Now take a moment to tune into your legs. What's happening in your legs? Are you feeling any tension? And again, just gently ask your legs to relax and let go.

Now notice your belly. Are you holding tension in your belly? And relax and let go.

Bring your attention to your chest. Are you holding tension in your chest? What about your back and shoulders? Just ask these parts of your body to relax and let go. Now notice any sensation you might have in your back and shoulders. Relax and let go.

How about your neck? Are you holding tension in your neck? Relax and let go.

What about your face? Is there tension in your face? Relax and let go.

Notice your whole head. Are you holding any tension anywhere in your head? Relax and let go.

Take a moment to scan your entire body, from the tips of your toes all the way up to the top of your head. Noticing any tension you might have anywhere in your body. Then, just take a moment to bring your attention to that part of your body and gently ask it to relax. See if there is any other part of your body that feels some tension. Again, focus there and gently allow it to relax. And now, in your mind, scan your body beginning with your head, moving all the way to your toes, noticing how you feel. And now slowly begin to take in the sounds in this room. Notice the floor you are lying on.

And slowly open your eyes and take a nice big stretch. Whenever you feel upset and sense your muscles getting tense, you can scan them, and then tell yourself, "Relax and let go."

Thanks for trying this out with me.

○○○ **AFTER LISTENING TO THE CD**

What to Do

- Help your child explore and reflect on what happened during the progressive muscle relaxation:

  How are you feeling right now? What did you notice as you were asked to relax different parts of your body? What parts of your body were easy to relax? What parts were hard to relax? How easy or hard was it to follow Mr. Goleman's directions? Did your mind drift to other things, or were you able to follow along until the end? Can you imagine using this technique when you are going about the regular things you do and you feel a false alarm coming on? When might it be useful?

  It's helpful if you can together commit to another time you'll try this progressive muscle relaxation within the coming few days.

- Introduce the reflection journal as a tool for regular drawing and writing, as a way to reflect during these quiet times together. You might say:

  When we take this quiet time together, I'd like to end it by taking some time to draw or write in a journal, so we can keep a record of what happened when we tried these things out. I will do this, too. I have two journals here. We can personalize our journals any way we want.

  Let's take a few minutes and write or draw separately about how we felt about this experience and anything that we learned that we want to remember. Then we can both share what we have written or drawn if it feels comfortable to do that.

- When you both have finished, you can explore whether sharing your journal entries feels appropriate or not. See if there are any questions you would like to ask each other to better understand how this experience was for each of you.

- Ask whether your child would be willing to set another date with you to learn one more calming technique:

  Each time we take this special quiet time together, we'll do some activities and have a conversation. Then we'll listen to the CD and talk about what happened and draw or write in our journals. Once we have learned how to do the different calming activities that are on the CD, we'll probably just use the CD and our journals and take our quiet time perhaps sometimes together and sometimes separately. There is another technique on the CD that is different from this one. It focuses more on training the mind. Are you willing to give this another try? Can we make a date for when it might be possible to do this again?

- End by explaining that you would like to close this special time together the same way that you started — by ringing a bell to signal the start of a moment of silence — and ask that you both close your eyes and then open your eyes when you no longer hear the bell.

- Ring the bell.

Extensions into Daily Life

- Refer to Guiding Principle 5: Integrate Rituals and New Routines (Chapter 2) for ways to continue to incorporate and reinforce the exercises learned. For example, your peace corner might now include the CD *Building Emotional Intelligence* so your children can use it on their own whenever they need some quiet time.

- At this age, your child can begin to make a distinction between stress cues, triggers, and reducers. You have already discussed stress cues (refer to the checklist "How Do I Feel When I Am Stressed?" on page 104). Stress triggers are those things that are likely to cause someone stress. As you begin to explore each of your stress triggers, your child will notice that these are different for each person. Stress reducers are techniques and ways of being that help people manage their stress; see the box "Ideas That Can Help Reduce Stress" (page 120), which you might read out loud with your child. You can both explore which things from this list you already use. Then perhaps each week you might choose one new idea for reducing stress that you can commit to trying out. Check in with each other about your progress.

- If your child is a worrier, introduce the idea of a "worry box." At night, before she goes to sleep, ask if there is anything that she is worried about. Then have her write each worry on a slip of paper and put it in the worry box. (It's fine if your child does not want to share her worries out loud.) Once a month (perhaps the last day of the month), suggest that she open the box and read all the worries. Then she can make note of how she feels in the present moment about some of those worries. You might also suggest a ritual of tearing those worries up, emptying the worry box, and beginning again the next day to collect the worries of the next month. You might decide that you also will have a worry box. You can both decide how comfortable you are sharing the details at the end of each month. You can also do the ritual by silently reading your own worries, sharing whatever feels comfortable to share, and witnessing each other tearing up the worries of the month.

• Both of you can be on the lookout for inspirational quotes that can be put in your child's room or carried in her pocket. Suggest she repeat one of these quotes to herself a few times a day. Here are a few suggestions:

"This above all: to thine own self be true."

— *William Shakespeare*

"All our dreams can come true,
if we have the courage to pursue them."

— *Walt Disney*

"Life is 10 percent what you make it and
90 percent how you take it."

— *Irving Berlin*

• Using a compass, ask your child to draw a big circle on an 8½" × 11" piece of paper, dividing the circle into six equal parts. Label the parts: school, health, family, friends, helping others, relaxation. If you are doing this yourself, substitute the word "work" for school. Place a dot in each part showing how happy or satisfied you are with this segment. If you are very satisfied, your dot would be near the outer rim of the circle. A dot near the center of the circle would mean that you are not very satisfied. Then connect the dots. Show each other your drawings and discuss what you see. How balanced do each of your lives look?[3]

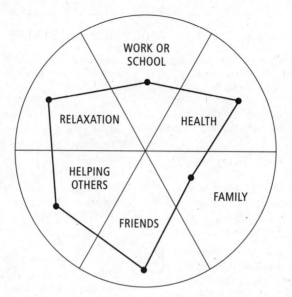

- Instead of using a worry box, when you say good night to your child, have an evening ritual of naming each of your concerns as you hold them one by one in a tightened fist. Then release your hand and let those concerns simply float away. You might end with sharing moments from your day that you felt good about or that put a smile on your face.

  When taking a long car trip or at other times when you and your child might be in a confined space for a while, talk her through a shortened version of the progressive muscle relaxation experience by simply using a few words as cues. For example, you might say:

  Hands — squeeze . . . and release . . . feet and legs — squeeze . . . and release . . . stomach — squeeze in . . . and release . . .

IDEAS THAT CAN HELP REDUCE STRESS

- Use positive self-talk. When you want to calm down, remind yourself that whatever is happening is not really an emergency. You might say to yourself, "Breathe. This is not a real emergency, and I can deal with this."
- Take a bubble bath or a warm shower.
- Read a small portion of a good book each day at a certain time.
- Listen to a piece of your favorite music.
- Draw, paint, or make a collage.
- Color in a mandala using *Everyone's Mandala Coloring Book #1* (see the Materials Checklist to order this item).
- Take a walk.
- Exercise, do some yoga poses, or dance.
- Take time in nature to look at the clouds, smell the flowers, or listen to the birds.
- Cook or bake something you love to eat.
- Watch an inspirational or funny movie.
- Cuddle with a pet and/or walk the dog.
- Say no to doing some things, so your plate doesn't get so full that there is not enough free time for things you like to do.
- Do something that has repetitive movement, such as jumping rope, knitting, or chopping vegetables.
- Do some gardening.
- Work on a puzzle that has lots of pieces—how about 1000!
- Sing out loud.
- Use earplugs when you want to cut down the noise.
- Visualize a quiet, peaceful place, like a beach, and go there in your imagination.
- Write in a journal and/or write yourself an e-mail or a letter encouraging yourself about something that concerns you. Mail the letter to yourself.
- Do some deep breathing, counting slowly to five on the in breath and backward on the out breath. Repeat at least seven time to feel yourself relaxing.
- Take time out to practice one of the calming techniques on the *Building Emotional Intelligence* CD.
- Start counting backward from 100 by threes.
- Go swimming.
- Ride a bike.
- Have a joke book handy that you can take out and read when you need a good laugh.
- Spend quality time with a good friend.
- Play a sport.
- Have a hobby and make time to do it regularly.
- Spend quality time with an adult you can trust and talk to.
- Play with a young child.
- Do a crossword puzzle.
- Build something.
- Make a list of the things in your life for which you are grateful.
- Volunteer or do something positive to address a concern you have about the world.
- Your idea _____

    _____

    _____

EXERCISE

PAYING ATTENTION: MINDFULNESS

This exercise is Track 6 on the CD.

In this session, young people will be introduced to the practice of mindfulness, which quiets the mind and focuses attention using the breath as a focal point. Mindfulness is a way of paying attention to the present moment without judgment. You'll help your child bring his full attention and focus to doing some simple everyday activities, as well as a few fun and challenging ones. Then your child will experience feeling more mindful directly by bringing his full attention to the process of eating an orange in slow motion, noticing how it feels in the present moment. The guided experience of mindfulness on the CD will introduce your child to the breath as an anchor for bringing his wandering mind back to attention. Then you'll explore ways to build mindfulness into your everyday life as you both record your experiences in your journals.

○○○ **BEFORE LISTENING THE CD**

What You'll Need

☐ Bell/chime

☐ A timer

☐ Two oranges (tangerines or bananas work, too) and a napkin for each person

☐ A tray of about fifteen everyday objects — e.g., a rubber band, a pen, a dollar bill, toothpaste, a screwdriver, a stone, a spoon, a key, a paper clip, a photograph, a cup of water half full, scissors, a piece of fruit, a Band-Aid, a can opener (When preparing the tray, leave room between the objects so that each one can be clearly seen, but don't necessarily line them up. Cover the tray.)

☐ A piece of paper and a pen for your child

☐ Two reflection journals, and pens, crayons, or colored markers

☐ A straight-backed chair for each person

☐ Biodot card

☐ The book *Building Emotional Intelligence*

☐ A CD player and the CD *Building Emotional Intelligence* cued up to "Paying Attention: Ages 12 and Up"

Time You'll Need: 35 Minutes

Concepts and Skills

Young people will:

• articulate the meaning of "mindfulness" as "paying attention on purpose, without judgment, moment-to-moment"[4]

• experience mindfulness, as opposed to the mind being on automatic pilot

• practice quieting the mind by using the breath as an anchor to bring attention to moment-to-moment awareness

• develop strategies for dealing with distractions during periods of stillness by learning how to name thoughts that come and go

What to Remember

- The thoughts, feelings, and sensations that come up during a mindfulness activity are not considered distractions. They are welcomed without judgment and become part of the experience.

- Young people can learn to think of their breath as an anchor or home base. While the minds may drift like a boat, they can always return to the awareness of their breath as a way of bringing their attention to the present moment.

- During a mindfulness experience, it is useful to label thoughts that come and go, using simple words like "hearing," "thinking," and "feeling." This process helps young people to notice where their attention is, so they can then bring themselves back to their breath.

- Mindfulness can be practiced by sitting still and/or as a habit of awareness to cultivate during regular daily life. That is, we can approach any daily task — such as brushing our teeth, dressing, and eating — with the kind of full attention and wholeheartedness cultivated in mindfulness.

Setting the Stage

- Remind your child that you would like to begin each session with a moment of silence. Explain that you will ring the bell once. Ask your child to close his eyes and then open his eyes when he doesn't hear the bell anymore. Ring the bell.

- You'll explore the concept of mindfulness through two challenge games that require you to be fully aware. Explain that this next exercise will help your child quiet his mind and strengthen his ability to pay attention. You might introduce the session this way:

  Today I'd like to try out another calming technique that will help quiet our minds and improve our concentration. In fact, it helps us to do a lot of things better, and it's called "mindfulness." Mindfulness simply means being aware of what you are feeling or thinking in the present moment, paying attention on purpose to what you are feeling or thinking right, now and paying attention to what you are doing as you are doing it — without judging or worrying about it. On any day of our lives, we do a lot of things without really noticing what we are doing — especially if we do them every day — like brushing our teeth or eating. Our minds are not really focused on what we are doing a lot of the time. For example [look at a clock], *it is about _____ o'clock right now. Let's see if we can remember what we were doing yesterday at this time. What about a week ago?* [Pause to discuss.]

- You may make the point that we often think we remember everything, but don't. Increased focus on paying attention to the present moment can help us to do that. Explain:

  When we are mindful, we bring our full selves and whole heart to any daily activity. Learning how to quiet our minds helps us to focus our attention better, and that improves our concentration and ability to learn new things.

Play a Couple of Challenge Games

- Introduce the activity:

  I'd like to try out a fun activity with you now to explore what it feels like to be mindful and really concentrate on what you are seeing. It's a memory game.

- Have the tray of fifteen everyday objects available, but still covered. Explain the game:

  In a moment, I am going to show you a tray that has several objects on it, and I am going to give you one minute to look at the objects. You can't touch them or write down anything during this minute. Remember, this is just a fun game. It is meant to get you some practice in really concentrating. After the first minute I will ring the bell and cover the objects. You will have a few more minutes to write down as many objects as you can remember. Then we will take a look and see what happens.

  You might decide to do this twice: give your child another look and ask for a second list while you hold the first one. You could have a discussion first to see whether he tried to remember the objects by working out a system. Usually, your child will do a lot better with the second list.

- Give your child a pen and paper. Take the cover off the tray and begin!

- Have a discussion afterward about how difficult it is to stay focused and train our minds to pay attention. However, with practice, we can train our minds to concentrate better, and that is what the concept of mindfulness helps us with. Summarize and introduce the next activity:

    Being mindful means bringing all your attention to something. These different experiences we are trying out today require us to bring all our attention to the task we were doing: remembering what we did yesterday or creating the list of objects you saw. We had to be mindful and really pay close attention. Now I'd like to try one more experience of mindfulness with you before we listen to the CD. This may seem a little strange, so bear with me.

Mindfully Eating an Orange

- Explain that you are going to set a timer for three minutes, which may seem like a long time at first. During this time, each of you will begin to eat an orange (or tangerine or banana) in slow motion, taking only a couple of bites from it in the three minutes. Encourage your child to stay in the present moment, touching the orange, smelling it, slowly peeling it, and finally taking a couple of bites, noticing the taste in his mouth, how it feels on his tongue, and then slowly chewing that one piece and swallowing it and then another. Remind him that you will be doing this entire experience in slow motion and that you are trying to let the experience last the full three minutes and that you will each do this without speaking.

- Afterward, ask:

    So what was that like? What did you notice? Any surprises? Was that hard or easy to do? Why?

    Share your own insights.

○○○ **LISTENING TO THE CD**

(Have the CD ready, cued to "Paying Attention: Ages 12 and Up," for the next part of the activity.)

- Introduce the "Paying Attention: Mindfulness" exercise, an experience your child will be led through by Daniel Goleman.

    So far we've experienced different ways of being mindful. Now, for the second time, we'll be listening to the CD where the man named Daniel Goleman will be leading us through another experience of training our minds to pay attention as our bodies relax. This time we will be sitting still in our chairs and noticing what we are thinking and feeling each moment. He is going to tell us about using our breath to help us focus our attention.

    If you choose to use biodots, you can ask the following:

    Would you like to put your biodot on during this time? What color do you think it will be? Let's see.

    With or without a biodot, you can continue:

    Are we ready to turn the CD on?

- Have your child and yourself put on a biodot, if appropriate, then get comfortable in your chairs and start the CD.

Paying Attention: Mindfulness (CD Script)

For ages twelve and up: 13:51 minutes

The method for training the mind we are about to experience is called "mindfulness." It's both a calming technique and a way to learn to pay attention better.

In this session, our task is simply to notice what's happening at any given moment. We don't try to control our thought process, but just to be aware of it. We simply notice what's going on in our minds.

When you notice your thoughts come and go, the key is to use your breath as an anchor to help you focus and center yourself. Then, whenever you become aware that something has captured your attention, you can silently note it to yourself, and label what's going on in your mind using simple words. You might say to yourself, "Thinking" or "Feeling" or "Hearing" — and then, when it no longer holds your attention, return to being aware of your breath.

So let's begin.

Sit comfortably in a chair that has a firm straight back, in a quiet place where you won't be interrupted. Sit with your back straight but relaxed, with your hands comfortably on your lap. You can fold them or simply place them on your knees.

It's important to be comfortable yet alert and attentive, trying to keep as still and awake as possible during this session. You don't want to try this on a comfy couch, for example, because you might be tempted to doze off.

Now gently close your eyes.

Begin to notice your breath . . . Take a couple of deep breaths, letting both your chest and your belly rise on the in breath and letting your whole body relax on the out breath as your chest and belly fall . . .

Now start to let your breath go in and out naturally . . .

As you breathe in . . . and out . . . let your mind begin to settle and your body relax . . .

When you breathe in, you can silently whisper to yourself, "In . . ."

Each time you breathe out, you can silently say to yourself, "Out . . ."

Let each breath relax and refresh you, allowing it to have its own natural rhythm . . . in . . . out . . . in . . . out . . . Belly rising . . . Belly falling . . .

And now if your mind wanders from your breath, notice what's caught your attention. Perhaps you notice a sound outside or in the room or even in your body. Wherever your mind has wandered, just simply notice what's going on and silently name it. For example, you might say to yourself, "Hearing . . ."

While the thought continues, keep naming it to yourself: "Hearing . . ." "Hearing . . ."

Keep naming it softly: "Hearing . . ."

Notice what happens as you name it. Is it getting stronger, weaker? Is it fading away?

Then, as the sound fades from your attention, gently guide yourself back to your breath . . .

Notice the sensation of your breath at your nostrils, or notice your belly rising and falling.

In . . .

Out . . .

In . . .

Out . . .

If your mind wanders again and you begin to focus on a sensation in your body, name it — "Feeling" — until the sensation fades from your thoughts . . . and then come back to your breath . . .

If you are having some feeling arise in your mind, just think to yourself its name. Maybe it's anger or happiness. Just note the feeling — don't judge it, just be aware of it . . . and name it . . . Anger or happiness or whatever . . .

And in the same way, as soon as the feeling starts to fade, return your attention to your breath . . .

Don't worry about finding the exact right word to note where your mind has wandered — that's not important. Just use simple words like thinking, hearing, feeling, daydreaming. The naming should be in back of your mind like a whisper . . .

Whenever your mind wanders, remember to use your breath as an anchor. Return to your breath as other thoughts come and go . . .

It's okay if your mind drifts — just be aware where it has gone. Say to yourself whatever's happening in your mind — thinking, feeling, hearing, whatever. Then bring your mind back to your breath . . .

Just remember to name whatever comes into your mind that takes your awareness away from your breath, and make a silent note in back of your mind: thinking . . . or feeling . . .

Always return to your breath as the thoughts come and go from your mind . . .

Use simple words to label what you notice, and then continue naming it, and then come back to your breath and note . . .

In . . .

Out . . .

In . . .

Out . . .

Rising . . .

Falling . . .

It's fine for your mind to wander away from the breath — as long as you are aware of where your mind has drifted and then bring it back to your breath . . .

Keep the noting as a soft whisper in back of your mind . . .

Always remember to gently guide yourself back to your breath as other thoughts come and go . . .

Now, whenever you feel ready to stop, slowly open your eyes and notice how you are feeling right now.

As you go about your day, you can try a mindful moment or two whenever you want — it's a really good idea if you're feeling stressed, want to relax, or need to focus on what you're doing.

Thanks for trying this out with me.

○○○ **AFTER LISTENING TO THE CD**

What to Do

• Share how the experience of mindfulness was for both of you. Possible debriefing questions:

  So, how was that for you? Were you able to stay with Mr. Goleman's voice, or do you think your mind may have gone somewhere else?

  How easy or hard was it to name where your mind went?

  Share what sounds you both heard and what other labels you gave your thoughts that came and went.

  Was it easy or hard for you to keep bringing your mind back to your breath?

  On a scale from 0 to 10, with 0 being not hard to do at all and 10 being very hard, how would you rate this experience?

  Summarize any comments or insights and share what happened for you as well.

• Now pull out your reflection journals and remind your child how this special journal is one way that you both can reflect on what you've learned during your time together and what you want to remember.

  Let's take a few minutes to draw or write about today's experience. Let's try to capture any awareness or thoughts or feelings we experienced either while listening to the CD or trying out some of the other exercises. Let's both write or draw for about three minutes and then we'll see how we feel about sharing it with each other.

• Discuss a few ways that your child might be able to be mindful — or really pay close attention — to something he does all the time — a daily routine, perhaps. You might ask your child to think of something he is going to do before he goes to sleep tonight that he could do mindfully, e.g., brush his teeth. Ask:

  Are you willing to make another date to do either of the exercises we practiced? Can we each think of something we can commit to doing mindfully before we go to bed tonight?

- Finally, ring the special bell and ask your child to close his eyes and then open his eyes when he no longer hears it. Thank the child for spending this special time together and being willing to be open-minded about it.

Extensions into Daily Life

- Coloring can be a soothing and calming activity for children this age. You can try the *Everyone's Mandala Coloring Book #1* by Monique Mandali. Mandalas are geometric or symbolic patterns, usually in the form of a circle. Coloring these circles fosters the focused attention of mindfulness.

- Encourage your child to go on a mindfulness walk in nature or around your neighborhood. You can do this with him, or encourage him to do it alone. Plan a designated time period to walk in silence, simply noticing the smells, sounds, and sights you pass. For a first time taking this sort of walk in nature, it's helpful to focus your child's attention on the present moment by deciding together on one thing you may particularly look for. Depending on the season, it might be spiderwebs or ladybugs. Or, if you're walking on a city street, it might be a certain color or make of car. Suggest that you walk in silence, but either of you could point if you spot the special thing you are looking for.

- Introduce a "mystery smells" game. Have four or five herbs and spices that you commonly use, with their labels and containers covered and a blindfold available. In this game, your child will first smell each herb or spice — one at a time. Ask him to smell each one and, if he can, identify it. If he can't, introduce him to the name of the herb or spice and how you have used it in the past. For example, you might say, "This is rosemary, and I sometimes put it on baked chicken." After going over all of them, he can begin to play the mystery smells game by smelling each herb or spice one at a time with his eyes closed (or with a blindfold on) and trying to name what he is smelling. Give your child a few minutes to just smell and see if he can guess what each one is. After he has tried to guess all four or five herbs or spices, take off the blindfold and discuss.

- Think about transitions in your adolescent's life as a special opportunity to slow down the pace and mindfully honor that transition by doing something together as a family. Take the time to reflect on the particular change this transition will bring to his life by doing a ritual. It's helpful to get your child involved in creating whatever this ritual will be. Bringing a small group of loved ones together who are willing to share what this particular transition was like for them—e.g., entering middle school or high school—is one way to honor an important transition. Let your child take time to share some qualities or ways of being he feels are needed for success in this transition. You can then offer a blessing you have for him.

  You could also have your child choose an activity that you do together, such as a favorite meal or going to a favorite place, at that time of his life.

- Buy your child a snow globe. Suggest that she shake the ball and imagine that those little snow particles are all the thoughts in her mind. Encourage her to use it as a way of taking a mindfulness break, by watching it closely until every last particle settles to the bottom, leaving the mind as clear and calm as the water.

- So often in our harried days with our children, it can be easy to not have time to really be present with one another. The next time your child is telling you about his day, or is absorbed in a task, or is simply sitting near you, give yourself the gift of a mindfulness break. Stop and be present to whatever you can learn about who your child truly is.

Story Time

Although children this age are less likely to buy into the idea of reading a book together, finding the right book, which conveys some of the messages embedded in these lessons, can make the difference in coaxing your child into this precious vestige of childhood. Nothing can quite take the place of reading a good book out loud together. It can be calming, comforting, and inspiring. It is a powerful opportunity to bond and share in the delight of a good story.

The following list gives books recommended for this age in *Valerie and Walter's Best Books for Children: A Lively, Opinionated Guide,*[5] chosen for age-appropriateness and themes that are aligned with those in this book. While many of these books are picture books and might appear to be for younger readers, they share universal and sophisticated themes that are appropriate for young and old alike. Simply acknowledging to your child that a book might appear to be for younger kids, but is, in fact, even appropriate for adults, will do a lot to defuse concerns that a book is too "babyish" for your adolescent. You never are too old to be read to!

All the Way to Lhasa: A Tale from Tibet by Barbara Helen Berger. This beautiful tale of perseverance follows a small boy and his yak on a difficult journey to the holy city of Lhasa.

Holes by Louis Sachar. This story of perseverance, friendship, and the importance of family comes highly recommended from young people themselves. Complete with curses, prophesies, and assorted tales of redemption.

Joyful Noise: Poems for Two Voices by Paul Fleischman and Eric Beddows. This "guide to the insect world" can be read together out loud, creating a musical duet.

The Phantom Tollbooth by Norton Juster, illustrated by Jules Feiffer. This tale chronicles the adventures of a boy named Milo, who takes a delightful imaginary journey through a tollbooth in his room and jumps into the island of Conclusions.

The Three Questions: Based on a Story by Leo Tolstoy by Jon J. Muth. This provocative book explores Tolstoy's three questions: (1) When is the best time to do things? (2) Who is the most important one? and (3) What is the right thing to do?; and in the process, delves into the deeper purposes of life.

Weslandia by Paul Fleischman, illustrated by Kevin Hawkes. This book celebrates those who march to the beat of their own drum as it follows Wesley, who gains acceptance from his peers by building his own civilization.

CHAPTER 6

Preparing Children to Lead Us into the Twenty-First Century

What a precious gift children everywhere would have if they were equipped with some of the practical tools presented in this book! At any moment, children would be able to access these skills to help them with emotional regulation as well as to recover faster from stressful situations. The benefits are far-reaching—from better health and increased ability to learn, to more fulfilled and happier lives.

The emotional lessons about cultivating inner strength that children learn from the adults in their lives are powerful and long-lasting. When adults ignore their children's feelings, children come to believe their feelings are not important. When we repeatedly threaten or punish children for a display of emotion, children learn that emotions are dangerous things that need to be held inside and hidden—an invitation to later depression or rage. When adults are unable to show angry and destructive children other ways of expressing emotion and managing their feelings, children learn it is acceptable to strike out at others or have a tantrum to get what they want.[1]

A careful study of parental relationships and parents' interactions with children has shown another style of interacting that can help children grow in emotionally sound ways. Researcher John Gottman refers to this as being an "emotion coach."[2] This means that parents use opportunities presented by difficult or hurtful emotions, such as when a child has had an argument or experienced a disappointment, to explore the true nature of those feelings and how to work with them constructively. Parents can encourage children to use feeling words, such as "I feel sad" or "That made me really angry," to express their emotions rather than simply act on them. Children need ample opportunity to explore their emotional landscape with the caring adults in their lives.

Giving children a regular time to be in stillness can do much to help them make a safe passage from childhood to adulthood. When children are taught to appreciate silence and slow down, they have the rare opportunity to explore the deeper questions of life, such as "What is my unique purpose?" or "How can I best make use of my talents and gifts?" As both of you further explore how the mind works and pay closer attention to your thoughts, there is an opportunity to notice just what your beliefs, ideas, and feelings are. So often we don't have time to reflect on these things. We go on automatic pilot and don't register the deeper meaning of what we are experiencing.

One parent, Laura Parker Roerden, who uses many of these techniques in her home with her three children, describes how the effects of teaching these skills may not be immediate but often catch us by surprise, just when we think our efforts are not working. Driving in city traffic with her five-year-old son, Eli, Laura was starting to get very stressed herself when she heard from the back seat his reminder, "Just breathe, Mommy. Just breathe." And while synchronizing her breathing to her son's in their precious quiet moments of paying attention together before bedtime, Eli often reveals just how tuned into his own inner life he is. Many months after his grandfather passed away, Eli had this to say to his mom, seemingly out of the blue, during one of those quiet times:

"Mom," he said thoughtfully, breaking their silence, "I think that heaven is in my heart."

"Why do you think that, sweet pea?" his mother asked.

"Because Grandpa Parker is in heaven, and he's in my heart right now."

When children like Eli grow up in homes and schools that welcome the exploration of their inner lives, they are more likely to develop a healthy identity filled with love, hope, and optimism. Children who are able to self-reflect and calm themselves are more capable of recognizing, identifying, and managing their emotions. They can also concentrate and think more clearly. Distress is less likely to spill over into antisocial behavior. Children are then able to bring their full attention, enthusiasm, interest, and positive emotional response to any situation. As a result, their full potential can be reached.

For example, when children notice the flow of their feelings, thoughts, or sensations while they are experiencing one of these calming exercises, they are developing the ability to use that awareness at any time in their lives. When they get upset and are not sure what is happening for them, they may first be able to use one of these techniques to begin to gain control of their emotions and calm themselves down. It is a lot easier for children to talk about what they are upset about when they are able to get out of the "stress response" mode. If they are able to notice where in their bodies they feel this upset, they can use their minds to let go of it enough to be able to talk about it and even think of some ways they might solve the situation or feel better about it.

As we begin to work with these kinds of approaches with children, we have to root this work in scientific research, as well as in sound pedagogy and child-development theory. Most child-development theory has focused on personality development and on the emotional and intellectual realms; only rarely does it consider the inner or intuitive dimensions of experience. However, we can't think about giving our children these skills and ways of being without getting support in the nurturing of our own inner lives. Many of us want to help our children find deeper purpose and meaning, but we can't give what we don't have. Soul work isn't about giving our children a road map. It must flow from the quality of our own inner lives.

What a legacy we can leave our children, by offering them concrete ways to strengthen the core of who they are! If as children they learn to honor silence, self-reflection, and going within, this way of being can follow them for the rest of their lives. It can become a daily practice for them to take a "heart and soul" time for themselves. I was actually in my early twenties when my mother suggested one day that we both go together to be initiated in a certain meditation technique. Since that day in 1971, I have made it a daily practice to take a time of silence and stillness with myself in meditation. If it had not been for my mother suggesting this and doing it with me, I am not sure I would have opened myself up to this possibility. Learning these techniques was a breakthrough in my life, and the habit has remained to this day. These skills continue to be one of the most important inner resources I rely on to bounce back from setbacks and losses.

Many courageous educators and parents are breaking new ground and teaching children these contemplative skills. In 2002, when we started to teach children these calming strategies in the New York City Schools, there were only a handful of such efforts. Today, there are many more efforts to bring contemplative practices into schools not only in the United States, but also across the world. We are learning that we can offer children some concrete, usable tools that can greatly improve the quality of their lives.

We mustn't put these strategies in the category of religious education, nor of exposing our children to particular devotional practices. Teaching children these calming strategies is an exciting and powerful way to attend to their inner lives, while respecting both the religious convictions of some and the more secular beliefs of others. We are talking about approaches that encourage a commitment to matters of the heart and spirit, which are among the positive building blocks of healthy development.

For example, in Susan Soler's second-grade classroom in New York City, children not only learn to honor silence, they know when to ask for it as well. One day, after teaching her children several lessons from our curriculum, Susan was trying to get their attention as they were very noisy and the next activity required them to really concentrate. She said to her class, "I'd like to hear a pin drop." The children grasped this idea and went with it for the whole year. Whenever it was difficult for them to concentrate and focus their attention on the task at hand because of the noise or hurried pace of the moment, any child could say to the class, "I need a pin drop." The class would take a minute of silence by ringing a bell at the beginning and end of a minute, in order to regroup.

In fact, Susan tells me that she never used that bell to get her students' attention—she used maracas. The special bell signified "inner peace," as the children started to call this silence and stillness time. When the assistant principal stopped by for a visit one day, one of the children said, "Let's give Ms. Regina a gift of inner peace"—and all the children knew that meant a minute of silence, as the bell was rung by one of the students. This classroom integrated these tools throughout their school day in a number of other ways. For example, several of the children dealt with one very argumentative child, who was often not in control of his emotions, by taking some deep belly breaths on their own as a way to gain more patience so they would not have a reactive response to him. They also put to use a skill of taking other people's perspectives. However, had they not been able first to calm themselves down, it might have been harder for them to access the skill of perspective taking that they had learned earlier.

THE OPPORTUNITY WE HAVE

As we move forward, we are holding in our individual and collective hands the opportunity to use our civilization's new knowledge and advances for unbearable evil, devastation, and moral breakdown— or for goodness, transformation, and hope. The choices we make today regarding how we nurture our children's development will have critical implications for generations to come. Even as we make huge advances in the world of technology and our understanding of the brain, in this country we are struggling to rescue generations of young people who are growing up without the support they need to feel valued and to participate meaningfully in their communities.

Take a moment to think about each one of the children who is a part of your life, and ask yourself what is it you really want as a parent or teacher for these children. What are some of your hopes for them? A variety of answers will arise, depending on the particular needs, strengths, and challenges of the child you are thinking of. However, whether they will be successful at realizing those hopes is dependent on whether they are equipped with the inner strength to approach their day-to-day challenges and the big challenges life may throw them. Are they capable of being resilient in the face of obstacles, as well as opportunities? Can they bounce back and even surpass their level of coping when the tests of life come their way?

How successful will we be in nurturing children's inner lives and cultivating their inner strength? We adults need to let young people themselves show us how we can help them cultivate their inner lives. J. Robert Oppenheimer, one of the pioneers of nuclear energy, once said, "There are children playing in the streets who could solve some of the top problems in physics, because they have modes of sensory perception that I lost long ago."[3] Exploration, innovation, and creativity often come more easily to children. They are already interested in life's most basic questions. Our task is to remember how integrated our children's inner lives are and to find ways to protect them from being trampled on.

I am reminded of a wonderful story that my friend Martin Brokenleg told me from his Lakota heritage: An old Native American man was down on the ground interacting with a tiny child. His relatives said to him, "Grandfather, what are you doing crawling around on the ground like a little child?" He responded, "I am very old and some time soon I will be going to the spirit world. This child is very young and has just come from the spirit world. I am down here seeing what I can learn from this sacred being."[4]

This new focus on teaching children contemplative practices moves some of the key elements of emotional intelligence into a deeper dimension. Self-awareness takes on a new depth of inner exploration; managing emotions becomes self-discipline; empathy becomes a basis for altruism, caring, and compassion. And all these basic skills for life

can now be seen as building blocks of character. A window of opportunity exists right now in our society for these kinds of approaches
to make their way into our homes and our schools. It is essential for
children to learn new ways to have their human spirits uplifted and
their inner lives nourished as a normal, natural part of their childhood experience. Far from being marginal or irrelevant, attention to
building our children's emotional intelligence and inner lives will
help us achieve the equilibrium we all need in this chaotic world; we
must foster the compassion, insight, and commitment to ourselves
and each other that will be necessary to tackle the deep emotional,
social, political, and spiritual dilemmas of our time. And, as Gandhi
has reminded us, "We have to start with the children."

As I look at the huge problems our young people will inherit —
racism, poverty, terrorism, the degradation of nature — I can't imagine
how we will make it if we don't cultivate children's inner strength.
My hope is that each of us finds a way to act to make sure that no
child is left behind and that every aspect of the human spirit is nurtured in our homes, our communities, and our schools.

Finally, I would like to offer this invocation for the children of the
future, written by one of my friends and mentors, Angeles Arrien,
who has done much to nurture my own inner life:

INVOCATION FOR CHILDREN

May you be powerfully loving and lovingly powerful;
may you always have love be your guide with family,
friends, and colleagues. Remember to listen carefully
to your own heart and to the hearts of others.

May you have the courage to always follow your
dreams. Take an action every day to support your life
dream, your love of nature, and your integrity.

May you have the strength to overcome fear and pride, and
instead follow what has heart and meaning for you.

May you be guardians of truth, beauty, creativity, and laughter.

May you protect, preserve, and care for nature and the wilderness.

May you show respect to people of all ages and races,
and help all living things keep their dignity.

May you help to make a better world for the poor, the
sick, the elderly, and the young by being an active,
committed, and positive force in your community.

May you value and maintain your health and
the health and well-being of others.

May you respect all the ways human beings access their spirituality.

May you help create a global community
committed to peace and nonviolence.

May you keep learning; ask questions, explore, discover,
and always maintain curiosity and hope.

May you honor and respect diversity and the beauty
and magic that occur when differences join to create
something far greater than one can imagine.

May you bring your gifts and talents forward every
day without hesitation or reservation.

May you honor your ancestors and all those who
have gone before you, for they have paved the way
for you to do what you are here to do.[5]

My own hope for the children of the world is that more and more adults will provide them with the "internal armor" they need to have the inner resilience that Anne Frank wrote about in her diary in 1944: "I have a lot of courage, I always feel strong and as if I can bear a great deal, I feel so free and so young! I was glad when I first realized it because I don't think I shall easily bow down before the blows that inevitably come to everyone."[6]

May each of us find the courage to do our part in offering our children the very things they need to lead us into the twenty-first century.

Materials Checklist

Bell/chime   The bell can be a chime or a regular hand-held bell. We recommend the Meinl Energy Chime, single chime (large size), which can be obtained from Amazon.com, but any bell can be used.

Biodot card   Biodots are stress dots used to identify different levels of stress through a biofeedback mechanism. They can be obtained from www.stressstop.com.

Mandala Coloring Books

Kids Mandala Coloring Book Set (for children 8 to 11 years old) by Monique Mandali (available from Amazon.com or from the author at www.mandali.com).

Everyone's Mandala Coloring Book #1 (for 12 years and up) by Monique Mandali (available from Amazon.com or from the author at www.mandali.com).

Page Clamp book holder   We recommend you purchasing the FlipKlip to hold open the book as you use it with your child. It can be obtained from www. bluezap.com.

RECOMMENDED CHILDREN'S BOOKS

The following books recommended in Chapters 3–5 are available at many bookstores and libraries, as well as through Amazon.com:

All the Way to Lhasa: A Tale from Tibet by Barbara Helen Berger (Philomel Books, 2002)

Cherish Today: A Celebration of Life's Moments by Kristina Evans (Jump at the Sun, 2007)

Everybody Needs a Rock by Byrd Baylor (Aladdin, 1985) `

Holes by Louis Sachar (Yearling, 2003)

Joyful Noise: Poems for Two Voices by Paul Fleischman (HarperTrophy, 2004)

The Listening Walk by Paul Showers (HarperTrophy, 1993)

Peaceful Piggy Meditation by Kerry Lee MacLean (Albert Whitman, 2006)

The Phantom Tollbooth by Norton Juster (Random House, 2000)

A Quiet Place by Douglas Wood (Aladdin, 2005)

The Seashore Book by Charlotte Zolotow (HarperTrophy, 1994)

There's a Big, Beautiful World Out There! by Nancy Carlson (Puffin Books, 2002)

The Three Questions: Based on a Story by Leo Tolstoy by Jon J. Muth (Scholastic Press, 2002)

Weslandia by Paul Fleischman (Walker Books, 2007)

The Wonderful Happens by Cynthia Rylant (Aladdin, 2003)

Resources for Further Exploration of the Topics Presented

All Kids Are Our Kids: What Communities Must Do to Raise Caring and Responsible Children and Adolescents by Peter L. Benson (San Francisco: Jossey-Bass, 2006). The author focuses on how to build developmental assets in young people, based on support, empowerment, boundaries, constructive use of time, commitment to learning, positive values, social competencies, and positive identity.

Calm and Compassionate Children: A Handbook by Susan Usha Dermond (Berkeley, CA: Celestial Arts, 2007). Parents and teachers can explore ways to develop empathy and integrity in children as the authors provide practical strategies to foster children's concentration, joy, kindness, and love.

Calming Your Anxious Mind: How Mindfulness and Compassion Can Free You from Anxiety, Fear, and Panic by Jeffrey Brantley (Oakland, CA: New Harbinger Publications, 2007). This book reminds us to stop and pay attention to ourselves and the life we want to lead. It helps us practice being, not doing, and gives clear information on the physiology of the stress response.

Emotional Intelligence: Why It Can Matter More Than IQ by Daniel Goleman (New York: Bantam, 2005). This best-seller raised public awareness of the importance of emotions in healthy human development and redefined what it means to be smart, making the term "emotional intelligence" part of our daily language.

Emotionally Intelligent Parenting: How to Raise a Self-Disciplined, Responsible, Socially Skilled Child by Maurice J. Elias, Steven E. Tobias, and Brian S. Friedlander (New York: Three Rivers Press, 2000). Parents can learn how to communicate with children on a deeper, more gratifying level and support their child's development in relating to others.

Everyday Blessings: The Inner Work of Mindful Parenting by Jon Kabat-Zinn and Myla Kabat-Zinn (New York: Hyperion, 1998). The authors share how important the nurturing aspects of parenting are. They explain how moment-to-moment awareness can help parents slow down as they enrich their lives and nourish the internal lives of their children.

Forever After: New York City Teachers on 9/11 edited by Teachers College Press with Maureen Grolnick (New York: Teachers College Press, 2006). A wonderful collection of reflections from the unique perspective of schoolteachers in New York City who dealt with children's fears and recovery firsthand.

The Heart of Parenting: Raising an Emotionally Intelligent Child by John Gottman (New York: Simon & Schuster, 1997). The author describes how parents can use an effective five-step process to become "emotion coaches" and teach their children how to express and manage emotions throughout their lives.

Meditation for Beginners by Jack Kornfield (Boulder: Sounds True, 2004). The acclaimed author and respected meditation teacher distills the essential teachings of the art of meditation. A CD of six guided meditations for adults is included.

The Miracle of Mindfulness: An Introduction to the Practice of Meditation by Thich Nhat Hanh (Boston: Beacon Press, 1999). This accessible guide to Eastern meditation offers a method of exploring the skills of mindfulness that beginners can easily understand.

Parenting from the Inside Out by Daniel J. Siegel and Mary Hartzell (Los Angeles: Tarcher, 2004). The authors present a practical model of parenting that shows parents the need to integrate their own childhood experiences and how they shape their own parenting style.

Parenting with Spirit: 30 Ways to Nurture Your Child's Spirit and Enrich Your Family's Life by Jane Bartlett (New York: MJF Books, Fine Communications, 2004). The author presents, in practical detail, thirty tools to nurture children's inner lives, regardless of specific religious beliefs.

The Power of Relaxation by Patrice Thomas (St. Paul, MN: Redleaf Press, 2003). The author advocates for the importance of teaching self-quieting skills to children, and guides parents and teachers in how to offer them.

The Radiant Child by Thomas Armstrong (Wheaton, IL: The Theosophical Publishing House, 1985). The author makes the point that children come into life with their spiritual nature close to their awareness and encourages those who work with children to recognize this aspect in the child.

Raising Emotionally Intelligent Teenagers by Maurice Elias, Steven Tobias, and Brian Friedlander (New York: Three Rivers Press, 2002). The authors explain creative, caring, and constructive ways to parent adolescents during these crucial years.

Raising Resilient Children by Robert Brooks and Sam Goldstein (New York: McGraw-Hill, 2002). The authors discuss the qualities that resilient children possess, and offer specific ideas and strategies to develop a resilient mind-set.

The Relaxation and Stress Reduction Workbook—Fifth Edition by Martha Davis, Elizabeth Robbins Eshelman, and Matthew McKay (Oakland, CA: New Harbinger Publications, 2000). A comprehensive guide with clear instructions and background on many major stress-management approaches. A great self-help reference tool.

Schools with Spirit: Nurturing the Inner Lives of Children and Teachers edited by Linda Lantieri (Boston: Beacon Press, 2002). Fourteen respected educators discuss how schools can nurture children's inner lives without violating the beliefs of families or the separation of church and state.

The Secret Spiritual World of Children by Tobin Hart (Makawao, HI: Inner Ocean, 2003). The author combines his background in spirituality, psychology, and education to help parents and teachers recognize and develop children's spiritual capacities. He also helps adults remember their own childhood spiritual experiences.

Social Intelligence: The New Science of Human Relationships by Daniel Goleman (New York: Bantam, 200). The internationally respected author explores the implications of our interpersonal world through a new science of human relationships that offers a deeper understanding of how capacities of social intelligence are developed and nurtured in ourselves and others.

Taking Back Childhood: Helping Your Kids Thrive in a Fast-Paced, Media-Saturated, Violence-Filled World by Nancy Carlsson-Paige (New York: Hudson Street Press, 2008). In the fast-paced, consumer-driven, achievement-oriented society we live in today, how can we help our children grow to their full potential as human beings? This groundbreaking guide will help all those who care about kids to navigate the social currents shaping—and, too often, harming—the lives of kids today, so we can restore childhood to the very best it can and should be.

Tough Times, Strong Children: Lessons from the Past for Your Child's Future by Dan Kindlon (New York: Hyperion, 2003). Combining his clinical experience with psychological and biological research, the author explains the process children go through in dealing with adversity, and how they are able to survive and thrive.

Notes

Introduction

1. R. P. Weissberg, J. A. Durlak, R. D. Taylor, A. B. Dymnick, and M. U. O'Brien, "Promoting social and emotional learning enhances school success: Implications of a meta-analysis." Manuscript submitted for publication (2007).

Chapter 1: Building Inner Preparedness

1. These 9/11 stories are from the Foreword, Chapter 1, and Chapter 9 of *Forever After: New York City Teachers on 9/11*, edited by M. Grolnick and published by Teachers College Press, 2006. Used with permission.

2. P. Thomas, *The Power of Relaxation* (St. Paul, MN: Redleaf Press, 2003).

3. P. J. Rosch, "Job stress: America's leading adult health problem," *USA Magazine*, May 1991.

4. H. J. Eysenck, "Personality, stress, and cancer: Prediction and prophylaxis," *British Journal of Medical Psychology* 61 (1988), 57–75.

5. D. Wayne, "Reactions to Stress" (February 1998), available online at www.wovenstory.com/wellness.

6. D. Shafer, P. Fischer, et al., "The NIMH Diagnostic Interview Schedule for Children," *Journal of the American Academy of Child and Adolescent Psychiatry* 35 (1996) 865–77.

7. From http://kidshealth.org/parent/emotions/feelings/kids_stress.html.

8. Thomas Achenbach's study is described by D. Goleman in "The educated heart," *Common Boundary*, November/December 1995.

9. B. Bernard, *Resiliency: What We Have Learned* (San Francisco: West Ed, 2004).

10. "Mr. Mindfulness: Living in the Moment Is Tough, Even for the Idea's Leading Exponent. Just Ask Jon Kabat-Zinn," *Washington Post*, July 12, 2005, F1.

11. "Into the Well: Wherever You Go, Be Mindful," *Washington Post*, August 14, 2001, F3.

12. "Study Suggests Meditation Can Help Train Attention," *New York Times*, May 8, 2007.

13. J. Suttie, "Mindful Kids, Peaceful Schools," *Greater Good*, Summer 2007.

14. Parts of this section have been adapted from *Schools, Families, and Social and Emotional Learning: Ideas and Tools for Working with Parents and Families* by L. Fredricks, R. Weissberg, H. Resnik, E. Patrikakou, and M. U. O'Brien, published by the Collaborative for Academic, Social, and Emotional Learning (CASEL) and the Mid-Atlantic Regional Laboratory for Student Success. Available online at www.casel.org. Used with permission.

15. L. R. Huesmann and N. G. Guerra, "Children's normative beliefs about aggression and aggressive behavior," *Journal of Personality and Social Psychology* 72, no. 2 (1997), 408–419.

16. D. Goleman, *Emotional Intelligence* (New York: Bantam Books, 1995).

17. J. E. Zins, R. P. Weissberg, M. C. Wang, and H. J. Walberg, eds., *Building Academic Success on Social and Emotional Learning: What Does the Research Say?* (New York: Teachers College Press, 2004).

18. Collaborative for Academic, Social, and Emotional Learning, *Safe and Sound: An Educational Leader's Guide to Evidence-based Social and Emotional Learning Programs* (Chicago: CASEL, 2003).

19. L. E. Shapiro, *How to Raise a Child with a High EQ: A Parents' Guide to Emotional Intelligence* (New York: HarperCollins, 1997).

Chapter 2: Preparing to Teach Children Exercises to Calm the Body and Focus the Mind

1. T. Hart, *The Secret Spiritual World of Children* (Makawao, HI: Inner Ocean, 2003).

2. Ibid.

3. M. Elias and J. Clabby, *Social Decision-Making Skills: A Curriculum Guide for the Elementary Grades* (New Brunswick, NJ: Center for Applied Psychology, Rutgers University, 1989). Used with permission.

4. Adapted from S. Usha Dermond, *Calm and Compassionate Children: A Handbook* (Berkeley, CA: Celestial Arts–Ten Speed Press, 2007).

5. L. Lantieri, ed., *Schools with Spirit: Nurturing the Inner Lives of Children* (Boston: Beacon Press, 2001). Adapted from "Lessons of the Wild" by Laura Parker Roerden. Used with permission.

6. H. Benson and E. Stuart, *The Wellness Book* (New York: Fireside Books, 1992).

7. M. Davis, E. Robbins Eshelman, and M. McKay, *The Relaxation and Stress Reduction Workbook — Fifth Edition* (Oakland, CA: New Harbinger Publications, 2000).

8. A. Goldstein, *The Prepare Curriculum* (Illinois: Research Press, 1999).

9. J. Kabat-Zinn et al., "Effectiveness of a meditation-based stress reduction program in the treatment of anxiety disorders," *American Journal of Psychiatry* 149 (1992), 936–43.

Chapter 3: Exercises to Calm the Body and
Focus the Mind for Five- to Seven-Year-Olds

1. J. Wilde Astington, "Theory of mind goes to school," *Educational Leadership* 56, no. 3 (November 1998), 46-48.

Chapter 4: Exercises to Calm the Body and
Focus the Mind for Eight- to Eleven-Year-Olds

1. J. Garbarino, F. Stott, and faculty of the Erikson Institute, *What Children Can Tell Us* (San Francisco: Jossey–Bass, 1989).

2. C. Wood, *Yardsticks: Children in the Classroom Ages 4–12* (Greenfield, MA: Northeast Foundation for Children, 1994).

3. S. Bothmer, *Creating the Peaceful Classroom* (Chicago: Zephyr Press, 2003).

4. J. Cornwell, *Sharing Nature with Children* (Nevada City, CA: Dawn, 1998).

Chapter 5: Exercises to Calm the Body and
Focus the Mind for Twelve-Year-Olds and Up

1. P. J. Rosch, "Job stress: America's leading adult health problem," *USA Magazine,* May 1991.

2. S. Bothmer, *Creating the Peaceful Classroom* (Chicago: Zephyr Press, 2003).

3. Adapted from J. Zimmerman Rutledge, *Dealing with the Stuff That Makes Life Tough* (New York: McGraw–Hill, 2004).

4. Adapted from a definition used by J. Kabat-Zinn in *Full Catastrophe Living* (New York: Delta Publishers, 1990).

5. V. Lewis and W. Mayes, *Valerie and Walter's Best Books for Children: A Lively, Opinionated Guide* (New York: Avon Books, 1998).

Chapter 6: Preparing Children to Lead Us
into the Twenty-First Century

1. J. Gottman, *The Heart of Parenting: Raising an Emotionally Intelligent Child* (New York: Simon & Schuster, 1997).

2. Ibid.

3. Quoted in M. McLuhan and Q. Fiore, *The Medium Is the Message* (New York: Bantam, 1967), 93.

4. L. Lantieri, ed., *Schools with Spirit* (Boston: Beacon Press, 2001).

5. From L. Lantieri, ed., *Schools with Spirit* (Boston: Beacon Press, 2001). Used with permission.

6. A. Frank, *Anne Frank: The Diary of a Young Girl* (New York: Bantam Books, 1993).

About the Author

L inda Lantieri is a Fulbright Scholar, keynote speaker, and internationally known expert in social and emotional learning, conflict resolution, and crisis intervention. Currently she serves as the Director of The Inner Resilience Program (formerly Project Renewal), a project of the Tides Center, which is an initiative that equips school personnel with the skills and strategies to strengthen their inner resiliency in order to model these skills for the young people in their care. She is also the cofounder of the Resolving Conflict Creatively Program (RCCP). Started in 1985, RCCP is now one of the largest and longest running research-based school (K–8) programs in social and emotional learning in United States. Linda is also one of the founding board members of the Collaborative for Academic, Social, and Emotional Learning (CASEL).

Linda has forty years of experience in education as a former teacher, assistant principal, director of an alternative middle school in East Harlem, and faculty member of the Department of Curriculum and Teaching at Hunter College in New York City. She is the coauthor of *Waging Peace in Our Schools* (Beacon Press, 1996) and editor of *Schools with Spirit: Nurturing the Inner Lives of Children and Teachers* (Beacon Press, 2001).

About Sounds True

Sounds True was founded in 1985 with a clear vision: to disseminate spiritual wisdom. Located in Boulder, Colorado, Sounds True publishes teaching programs that are designed to educate, uplift, and inspire. We work with many of the leading spiritual teachers, thinkers, healers, and visionary artists of our time.

To receive a free catalog of tools and teachings for personal and spiritual transformation, please visit www.soundstrue.com, call toll-free 800-333-9185, or write to us at the address below.

The Sounds True Catalog
PO Box 8010
Boulder, CO 80306